Attitude
Is Your

It Colors
Every
Situation

JAMES W.
MOORE

DIMENSIONS
FOR LIVING

NASHVILLE

Attitude Is Your Paintbrush: It Colors Every Situation

Copyright © 1998 by Dimensions for Living

This book is printed on acid-free paper.

Library of Congress Cataloging-in-Publication Data

Moore, James W. (James Wendell), 1938-
    Attitude is your paintbrush : it colors every situation / James W. Moore.
    p. cm.
    ISBN 0-687-07670-6
    1. Christian life—Methodist authors. 2. Attitude (Psychology)—Religious aspects—Christianity. I. Title.
BV4509.5.M64 1998
248.4—dc21   98-2666
                                                  CIP

Study guide written by Sally D. Sharpe.

05 06 07— 15 14 13

MANUFACTURED IN THE UNITED STATES OF AMERICA

For our grandchildren,
who have taught us
that grandchildren are, indeed, grand

Contents

Introduction: Attitude Is Your Paintbrush . . .
It Colors Every Situation 7

1. The Attitude of Gratitude:
Stopping to Say Thanks 15

2. The Attitude of Compassion:
Lead with Your Heart 25

3. The Attitude of Confidence:
Sailing Under Sealed Orders 35

4. The Attitude of Determination:
"Take Dead Aim!" 45

5. The Attitude of Humility:
"Not All of This Is Me" 53

6. The Attitude of Perseverance: "Never Give Up!" .61

7. The Attitude of Open-mindedness: "Hiding Under
the Couch and Hissing at What's New" 71

8. The Attitude of Joy: "Them That *Has* Does!" . . .79

9. The Attitude of Faith:
The Necessary Ingredients 87

10. The Attitude of Trust: "Let Him Play His Song" .95

11. The Attitude of Commitment: "Be Strong" 105

12. The Attitude of Ownership:
    The Importance of Ownership 115

13. The Attitude of Hope:
    Rowing Against the Wind 125

Epilogue: You Can Take Your Own Atmosphere
    with You 133

Study Guide 135

Introduction
Attitude Is Your Paintbrush . . .
It Colors Every Situation

I APPEAL TO YOU THEREFORE, BROTHERS AND SISTERS,
*by the mercies of God, to present your bodies as a living
sacrifice, holy and acceptable to God, which is your
spiritual worship. Do not be conformed to this world,
but be transformed by the renewing of your minds,
so that you may discern what is the will of God—what
is good and acceptable and perfect.*

—*Romans 12:1-2*

Ann Turnage is a good friend of mine. She is an inspiration to me and to many, many others because of her
strong faith, her inner strength, her determination, and
her great Christian attitudes, which have enabled her, by
God's grace, to overcome a terrific hurdle. Ann Turnage is
a cancer survivor who is now dedicating her life—heart
and soul—to the difficult but necessary task of helping
other people fight this dreadful, frightening disease.

Ann has developed a cancer ministry, a cancer support
group called Can-Care. The mission of Can-Care is to
improve the quality of life for cancer patients and their
families, and its staff members do an incredible job in
doing just that.

When Can-Care sponsored its first National Cancer Survivors' Day luncheon, Ann was one of the speakers. In her speech she said something that touched my heart deeply, one of the finest and most quotable quotes I have ever heard. She was talking about the importance of having a good attitude in life, and she said this: "Attitude is your paintbrush; it colors every situation."

Isn't that a great thought? As I heard Ann say it, my mind darted back to something Dr. Viktor Frankl expressed some years ago in his fascinating book *Man's Search for Meaning*. Dr. Frankl, an Austrian psychiatrist, was a prisoner of war for a long period of time in Nazi concentration camps. During his imprisonment, he noticed something that intrigued him. He observed that some of the prisoners who looked physically strong and robust were actually weak because of their poor attitudes, whereas some others, who outwardly appeared to be frail and feeble, were amazingly strong because of their positive attitudes. These positive people became an inspiration to all in the prison camp.

In his book, Frankl wrote this marvelous paragraph:

> We who lived in concentration camps can remember the ones who walked through the huts comforting others . . . giving away their last piece of bread. They may have been few in number but they offer sufficient proof that everything can be taken from us but one thing: the last of the human freedoms—to choose one's own attitude in any given set of circumstances . . . to choose one's own way.

You know what Dr. Frankl was saying? He was saying, "Attitude is your paintbrush; it colors every situation."

This is precisely what the apostle Paul was underscoring in Romans 12 when he said this: "Present your bodies as a living sacrifice . . . to God" (verse 1). In other words, let serving God and trusting God be the attitude of your life. "Do not be conformed to this world" (verse 2). Don't be imprisoned by your circumstances. Don't let the world around you squeeze you into its mold. Rather, be God's servant, do God's will, and trust God to bring it out right. Or simply, let your attitude of unflinching commitment to God color every situation!

The apostle Paul was right. Viktor Frankl was right. Ann Turnage was right. Attitude is *so* important. Attitude determines who we are and how we live day to day.

To be more specific, there are three basic Christian attitudes that are crucial for the living of these days, attitudes that color every happening, every circumstance, every situation.

THE ATTITUDE OF GRATITUDE

Some years ago, while on a speaking engagement in another state, I was invited one evening to have dinner with a family in their home. When we sat down at the table, the mother called on four-year-old Christopher to say grace, the prayer of thanksgiving before the meal. She had whispered to me earlier that they were trying to teach the children how to pray—not just memorized prayers, but prayers of gratitude to God straight from the heart. As we took our places at the table, this conversation took place.

"Christopher, will you say grace tonight?"

"Oh, Mom, do I have to? I don't know how."

"Sure you do. It's your turn. Just thank God for our many blessings. Just tell God what you are grateful for tonight."

Then, like a scene from a Norman Rockwell painting, four-year-old Christopher began to pray. With one eye devoutly closed in prayer and the other eye discreetly open so that he could look around as he prayed, Christopher thanked God for everything in sight.

"Thank you, God, for the chicken, the roast beef, the brown gravy, the potatoes, the tomatoes, the cantaloupe, the slaw, the baked beans, the salt, the pepper, the knives, the spoons, the forks, the placemats, the tablecloth, the napkins . . . " and on and on he went, naming everything on the table. His brothers and sisters snickered. His mom and dad smiled, and their shoulders shook as they tried so hard to keep from laughing out loud as Christopher went on and on, with one eye still prayerfully closed and the other eye surveying everything in sight.

"Thank you, God, for the table, the chairs, the floor and the drapes, the tea, the ice and the sugar, the Sweet 'N' Low, the lemons, the ketchup . . . " Finally, Christopher thanked God for all the people at the table, calling them all by name. He ended by thanking God for his dog, Spot, who was under the table, pulling on Christopher's pants leg. He thanked God for everything he could see, except the carrots. (He told me later that he doesn't like carrots!)

When Christopher finished, his brothers and sisters— as only older brothers and sisters can do—began to tease him, but his mother and father thanked him graciously and bragged on him for his thoughtful prayer. As I sat there looking at this heartwarming scene, I thought to myself: "Isn't this beautiful? A four-year-old child learning the attitude of appreciation, the attitude of gratitude." That thankful attitude will serve him well in his lifetime.

The happiest people I know are the grateful people; the strongest, most fulfilled people I know are the thankful people. Those who have the attitude of appreciation are the most zestful and radiant people in all the world. Even in the most difficult circumstances of life, they know, because of their strong faith, that God is with them, and that because God is within, they cannot be defeated. They know that, ultimately, God will give them the victory, and for that they are grateful. It is this powerful, positive attitude of appreciation that colors every situation. The apostle Paul put it like this: "Give thanks in all circumstances; for this is the will of God in Christ Jesus for you" (1 Thessalonians 5:18). In everything, give thanks, Paul says. In all circumstances, give thanks. Whatever happens, give thanks.

But let me point out that Paul does not say to give thanks *for* everything. Rather, he says to give thanks *in* everything, and there is a world of difference between the two. Paul doesn't mean that we should give thanks for cancer or war or tragedy or suffering. But he does mean that in every circumstance, we can be grateful. Whatever comes our way, we can give thanks. Why? Because God lives. Because God loves us. Because God cares and shares life with us! The God of all the universe, the God who set the moon and stars in place, cares about you and me, and he will be with us and see us through come what may. *That* we can count on, and for that we can always be grateful. As Christians, the attitude of appreciation is our paintbrush; it colors every situation.

THE ATTITUDE OF COMPASSION

The word *compassion* literally means "with heart." It means to reach out to others with your heart. In a word, it means kindness.

Several years ago, a young girl came to see me. She was seventeen years old, and she and her mom were not getting along. "Mom is driving me crazy," she said. "As soon as I walk in, she starts in on me. Ever since Dad left, it's been this way. She's so tense. I know she's under a lot of pressure, but she's always fussing and griping at me. She doesn't like my clothes. She doesn't like my hair. She doesn't like my earrings. She doesn't like my music."

I said to her, "When your mom starts in on you, what do you do?"

"I scream back at her," she replied. "I run to my room, slam the door, and lock it; and I won't let her in. She bangs on the door and shouts at me through the door, and I shout back. I don't know what to do. I've tried everything!"

"Have you?" I asked her. "Have you tried the way of kindness?"

"Kindness? What do you mean?" she asked.

"Let me show you," I said. "When you get home tonight, where will your mother be?"

"Well," she said, "I have cheerleading practice, so it will be about 6:30 or so before I get there. She will probably be in the kitchen making dinner."

"Okay. When you get home, try this: Before she has a chance to say anything, run into the kitchen and say, 'Mom, I have something to tell you, and it's really important: I love you so much! I really do! I'm so proud of you. I'm so glad you are my mom. I'm glad we are a family. I know I drive you up the wall sometimes, but I don't mean to. I love you, Mom. I want you to know that. I think you are a really terrific person. We are a great team, and together we are going to make it. That's all! I just wanted to tell you tonight that I love you and that you are the most precious thing in my life.'"

The teenager said, "She'll think I'm crazy."

"That's all right," I said to her. "Try it anyway."

The next morning, the girl called me. "Jim," she said, "you won't believe what happened! I did it just the way we planned. I ran in and said, 'Mom, I love you so much!' and all those other good things. Mom started crying, and she hugged me so tightly. She forgot about work. She forgot about her problems. She forgot about our bills. She forgot about dinner. We sat down at the kitchen table and talked nonstop for three hours. It was one of the greatest moments of my life! Of course, we still have some work to do, but now we are closer than ever."

Isn't it amazing what the attitude of compassion—of kindness—can do? As one anonymous writer put it: "Kindness is a language that the blind can see and the deaf can hear" (*The Little Book of Love,* Dimensions for Living; page 3).

Compassion or kindness is another crucial attitude for a Christian, because it becomes our paintbrush and colors every situation.

THE ATTITUDE OF CONFIDENCE

We don't have to "run scared." We don't have to be anxiety-ridden. We can trust God. We can be confident. Someone once asked the noted minister Dr. Phillips Brooks why he was so serene and poised all the time. The questioner said, "Dr. Brooks, what is it about you that makes you so optimistic and confident about life?" I love Phillips Brooks's answer. He said, "I am a Christian!"

He was right, wasn't he? As Christians, we can be confident because God is with us, and nothing—not even death—can separate us from God and God's love. The psalmist expressed it beautifully: "I fear no evil [I am confident]; / for you are with me" (Psalm 23:4). Poet Arthur Hugh Clough, in "With Whom Is No Variableness, Neither Shadow of Turning," put it like this:

> It fortifies my soul to know
> That, though I perish, Truth is so:
> That, howsoe'er I stray and range,
> Whate'r I do, Thou dost not change.
> I steadier step when I recall
> That, if I slip, Thou dost not fall.

13

Gratitude, compassion, confidence; three great and helpful attitudes. In the pages that follow, we will look more closely at these and other key Christian attitudes that give us strength for the living of these days—because they color every situation.

1
The Attitude of Gratitude
Stopping to Say Thanks

*O*N THE WAY TO JERUSALEM JESUS WAS GOING THROUGH
*the region between Samaria and Galilee. As he entered a
village, ten lepers approached him. Keeping their
distance, they called out, saying, "Jesus, Master, have
mercy on us!" When he saw them, he said to them, "Go
and show yourselves to the priests." And as they went,
they were made clean. Then one of them, when he saw
that he was healed, turned back, praising God with a
loud voice. He prostrated himself at Jesus' feet and
thanked him. And he was a Samaritan. Then Jesus
asked, "Were not ten made clean? But the other nine,
where are they? Was none of them found to return and
give praise to God except this foreigner?" Then he said
to him, "Get up and go on your way; your faith has
made you well."*

—Luke 17:11-19

Our granddaughter Sarah is now an active three-year-
old—underscore *active*! She is always busy and always in
a hurry because at three years of age, she already realizes
that there are so many exciting things to do and see and
experience in this incredible world God has given us.

Just last week, Sarah interrupted her playtime just long enough to run into the kitchen in search of a midafternoon snack. Hurriedly, she said to her mother, "Banana, Mommy, banana!" Jodi, her mother, handed her a banana. Sarah quickly grabbed the banana and turned to rush back out of the kitchen. Before she took very many steps, however, her mother said, "Sarah, what's the magic word?" Sarah screeched to a halt, turned around, and said, "Please! Thank you! You're welcome!" And then, "I love you, Momma!" At this point, Sarah got a second banana—and a warm hug! The magic word Sarah's mother was looking for was *thanks*. She got more than that, but that was the word she was looking for, because she knows how important it is for us to learn how to stop and say thanks.

Thanks-giving, gratitude, appreciation—whatever you want to call it—is learned. We don't come into this world as grateful people. We come into the world selfishly screaming our demands. Now, please don't misunderstand me. I love babies. They are absolutely wonderful—one of God's greatest miracles. But anybody who has ever been around a newborn baby knows that babies come into this world self-centered and impatient. They come into the world screaming, "Hold me, feed me, burp me, change me, rock me, walk me, sing to me—and do it right now!" And this is okay, because they are babies and that's the only way they can communicate—indeed, the only way they can survive. But as time goes by, they grow up, and as they mature—if all goes well—they learn how to be grateful, how to be appreciative, how to say thanks.

The crowning virtue of life is gratitude, and one of the most dramatic signs of Christian maturity is the easy ability to say thanks. Immature people don't know how to be grateful because they've never grown up! They go through life screaming, "Where's mine? What's in it for me?" But

16

mature Christians have a special spirit that is so beautiful. It's called gratitude!

This is why one of the first things we do as Christian parents is teach our children how to say grace at the dinner table. What do you call it at your house? Saying grace? Asking the blessing? Returning thanks? Which one did you learn first? "Blessed art thou, O Lord, who gives bread to the hungry and satisfies our hearts with good things." That's a good one. Or how about this one: "O Lord, bless this food to the nourishment of our bodies and us to thy service." Or maybe you learned this Scottish prayer of thanksgiving: "Lord Jesus, as thou didst bless the loaves and fishes, bless these our humble little dishes." Or perhaps this one: "For health, strength, and daily food, we give you thanks, O Lord."

Fred Craddock told about spending a Saturday with his three-year-old granddaughter, Kristin. They went for a walk and played together at the neighborhood park. They saw acorns and flowers and rocks and sticks and squirrels and birds and butterflies. They had a wonderful morning and returned home in time for lunch. As the two of them sat down at the table, Kristin boldly announced to her grandfather that they should return thanks before eating and that she would do it. And then she said, "God is great; God is good. Let us thank him for our food. Amen." Her grandfather also said "amen."

Kristin looked at him and said, "Gramps, we've got to do it again."

"Why? What's the matter?" he asked.

She said, "You didn't hold your hands right!"

"Oh, I'm sorry," he said.

Then little Kristin got out of her chair, walked over to her grandfather, fixed his hands, and, like an instructor, said, "Gramps, if you don't hold your hands right, it won't work!"

When Fred Craddock told this story, he ended by saying this: "Do you know what? Listen! I held my hands right, and it worked! It worked! Kristin was grateful, and I was grateful! It worked!"

Isn't that beautiful? Someone had been teaching that three-year-old girl the importance of "stopping to say thanks," and it was serious business to her. It was crucial to her that it be done and be done right. "Stopping to say thanks"—how sacred that is; how appropriate that is! It is one of the key expressions of faith and one of the most dramatic emblems of spiritual maturity.

That's what this poignant incident in Luke 17, where Jesus heals the ten lepers, is all about. Jesus was on the border between Galilee and Samaria. As he entered a village, he heard these ten lepers screaming at him, begging for help. They had to scream out because, by law, lepers were required to stay some fifty yards away from all other human beings. From half-a-football-field-length away, they screamed out, trying to get Jesus' attention. Jesus gave them his attention—and then some.

He told them to go show themselves to the priests; and as they went, they suddenly realized that they were cleansed, made whole, healed, delivered from the despicable, debilitating disease and from their horrible, isolated, outcast existence. And they were so thrilled, so excited, so moved, so grateful that they all immediately turned around and ran back to thank Jesus for what he had done for them, right? No! Not quite!

Only one of them returned—the lone Samaritan in the group. The outcast among outcasts, he was the only one who stopped to say thanks. The nine others went their merry way. I know what you're thinking right about now: "Shame on those ungrateful nine! If I'd been there, if I'd been one of those cleansed lepers, I would have turned back and thanked Jesus!"

Sure you would have. Why don't you do it now? Has he cleansed you, saved you, delivered you? Have you really thanked him? So often we are like those nine lepers who forgot to say thanks. We are so busy, spread so thin. We are stretched out and stressed out. We are so frazzled with all the things we have to do, need to do, and want to do that we just can't find the time to stop and say thanks to our Lord for what he has done for us.

Stopping to say thanks is so important, so precious, so beautiful, so right. That's what this story is about. That's why we know of and respect this Samaritan, because he took the time to go back and fall down at the feet of Jesus and say thanks. Let me take the time to stop now and say thanks. I'm grateful for so many things; let me mention just a few. I'm sure you will think of others.

I'M GRATEFUL FOR THE CHRISTIAN CHURCH

A few years ago in Oklahoma, a young woman went to a support group in her church. She was having a rough time. She had lost her husband and now had the full responsibility for her three children. She felt so alone, and she was afraid that she wouldn't be able to give her three children what they most needed as they grew up. This is what she said: "If it were just me, I'd be okay. Sure, I'm hurting and I'm lonely, and I'll have to do without some things, but I can handle it just fine. It's my kids that I'm worried about. So many of their friends have new clothes to wear to school this year—and not just new clothes, but expensive designer clothes. There's no way I'll ever be able to afford things like that, and it hurts me to see my kids feel like they're out of place. And later, when it comes to college, I don't know what in the world I'll do. We're just barely making it now."

With that, her voice trailed off, and she began to cry.

Just then, an older woman went over and put her arm around her and tried to comfort her. She said, "You know, I can really relate to what you are feeling right now because twenty years ago, I was in the same predicament. I had lost my husband, I had four young children, and I wasn't even making $500 a month. But let me tell you something. We made it, the five of us, and I'm so proud of who and where my kids are today. I'd put them up against anybody's kids." And then she said this: "I have one piece of advice to give you. It's the best advice I know. You may not be able to give your kids designer clothes or sports cars or trips to Europe, but there is one thing you can give them that's better than all of that: You can give them the church! Make sure that you and your kids go to church and Sunday school every week. That might not seem like much to you right now, but I cannot tell you what a difference it will make in the long run. They'll receive something there that many kids don't have and that money can't buy, and it's something upon which they can build their lives for the rest of their days. Give them the church. It's the best gift you can give them! It's the best thing you can do for them!"

She was right, wasn't she? The church is one of God's greatest gifts to the world. Let me ask you something: What would our community be like, what would our world be like, what would life be like if we didn't have the church? I am so grateful for the Christian church and for all the good it does in our world.

I'm Grateful for the Christian Faith

There is a story about a monastery in Portugal that is perched high on a three-hundred-foot cliff. The only way the monastery can be reached is by a terrifying ride in a swaying basket suspended from a single rope pulled by several strong monks. One day an American tourist was about to ride up in the basket. However, he became very nervous when he noticed that the rope was quite old and frayed. Timidly, he asked, "How often do you change the rope?" One of the monks replied, "Whenever it breaks!"

Many people today treat faith like that. They never turn to faith until something breaks. But, thank God, there are others who realize that the Christian faith is a lifestyle that works in practical daily living. It is not just some last resort. It is the way to live. It is the way to relate to other people. It is the way to serve and honor God.

One of this generation's finest novelists was a man named Walker Percy. Percy became a Christian when he was thirty. He confessed his faith in Christ and joined the church and was a faithful member until his death. Many of his fellow writers and critics were harsh and critical of him. They mocked him and ridiculed him. They said he had "caved in" to religion. One of them said to him, "What do you mean by betraying your intellectual integrity and becoming a Christian? There are so many other options."

"What options?" Percy asked.

The critic said, "Well, there is Eastern philosophy or spiritualism or new-age thinking or secular humanism or astrology or materialism . . ." and the list went on and on.

Percy waited until the critic finished and then said, "That's what I mean." Percy believed with all his heart that those aren't options at all; that Jesus is the answer to our deepest yearnings; that Jesus is the one who gives our lives meaning; that Jesus is the one who brings us fully alive; that Jesus is the one who is the hope of the world; that Jesus is the one who can cleanse and deliver and save us.

I am so grateful for the Christian church, and I am so grateful for the Christian faith.

I'M GRATEFUL FOR THE CHRISTIAN GOSPEL

Some years ago, a little boy went into a pet shop. He wanted to buy a puppy. The owner whistled, and four cute, frisky little puppies came running into the room with tails wagging, yipping happily. Then another puppy came straggling in, dragging one hind leg.

"What's the matter with that puppy, Mister?" the boy asked.

"Well, Son, that puppy is crippled. We took him to the vet and found that he was born with a weak leg. The leg will never be right."

Quickly, the little boy pulled out his money and said, "I'll take him! He's the one I want!"

"But, Son, you don't seem to understand," said the owner. "That puppy is going to be crippled all his life. Why in the world would you want him?"

Just then, the little boy reached down and pulled up his pants leg, revealing an iron brace that held his twisted leg, and he said, "Mister, that puppy is going to need someone to help him. He's going to need someone who understands."

Now, let me ask you something: Where did that little boy learn how to love sacrificially like that? You know, don't you? He learned it in the Christian church. He learned it through the Christian faith. He learned it from the Christian gospel. He learned it from the one who went to the cross for you and me, from the one who was human enough to understand and divine enough to forgive.

I am grateful for so many things: family, friends, home, health, career. But I also want to "stop and say thanks" to God for the Christian church, the Christian faith, and the Christian gospel.

What about you? Why not stop and say a prayer of thanks right now for these and the many other gifts that God has given you. The attitude of gratitude is so important to have, for it colors every situation!

2

The Attitude of Compassion

Lead with Your Heart

*A*ND A LARGE CROWD FOLLOWED HIM AND PRESSED IN
*on him. Now there was a woman who had been
suffering from hemorrhages for twelve years. She had
endured much under many physicians, and had spent
all that she had; and she was no better, but rather grew
worse. She had heard about Jesus, and came up behind
him in the crowd and touched his cloak, for she said,
"If I but touch his clothes, I will be made well."
Immediately her hemorrhage stopped; and she felt in
her body that she was healed of her disease.
Immediately aware that power had gone forth from
him, Jesus turned about in the crowd and said, "Who
touched my clothes?" And his disciples said to him,
"You see the crowd pressing in on you; how can you
say, 'Who touched me?'" He looked all around to see
who had done it. But the woman, knowing what had
happened to her, came in fear and trembling, fell down
before him, and told him the whole truth. He said
to her, "Daughter, your faith has made you well;
go in peace, and be healed of your disease."*

—Mark 5:24b-34

David Halberstam has written a wonderful book on the decade of the 1950s. In *The Fifties* (Fawcett Books, 1994), he recalls *The Ed Sullivan Show* and its dramatic impact on our nation at that time. He points to that particular television program as a landmark of the fifties, and, of course, it was. Halberstam reminds us of some of those wonderful, humorous moments on live national television when Ed Sullivan would accidentally get his words mixed up and end up with "his foot in his mouth."

One night, for example, the great singer Sergio Franchi was a guest performer on the show. He sang Malotte's "The Lord's Prayer," after which Ed Sullivan came on stage and—as only he could do—said, "Come on, ladies and gentlemen, let's hear it for 'The Lord's Prayer'!" I can just see him saying that.

Taking a cue from Ed Sullivan, let me suggest that what this dramatic passage in Mark 5 is saying to us is simply this: "Let's hear it for compassion!" As I noted in the introduction, the word *compassion* literally means "with heart." It means to reach out to other people with your heart, and that kind of active love is one of the most powerful things in all the world.

Philip Anderson tells about a touching and heartwarming experience he had with his sister when he visited her at work one day. She was, at the time, a director of patient services for the children's unit of a large Southern California hospital. On that particular day, she was giving her brother a tour through the unit. Anderson said that as they walked along, they could hear the cry of a baby coming from one of the rooms.

Finally, they came to that room. When he saw that crying baby, his heart sank. He couldn't believe his eyes. The child, who was about twelve months old, was covered from head to toe with terrible bruises and scratches and scars. At first he thought the baby had been in a terrible accident, but when he got close enough to see the baby's legs, his heart sank even more because written in ink all over the baby's legs were horrible obscenities. The terrible truth was that the child had been the victim of its parents' abuse. Anderson's sister showed him terrible scars on the bottom of the baby's feet caused by cigarette burns. Can you imagine it? The parents had battered and abused their own child.

Anderson himself must have wanted to scream and cry. He just couldn't understand how anybody could be so cruel to a baby—or to any human being. But then his sister leaned over the crib and very carefully, very tenderly, very lovingly lifted the child, holding the baby close to her. At first the baby stiffened and cringed and screamed all the more, as if suspicious of every touch. But as she held the baby securely and warmly, spoke lovingly, and gently patted and rocked the baby, soon the baby began to relax and quiet down. And finally, in spite of wounds and hurts from past experience, the baby stopped crying altogether—all because of the power of compassion (*Illustrations Unlimited*, James S. Hewett, ed., Tyndale House Publishers, 1988; pp. 113–14).

As strange as this may sound, that battered baby reminds me of the sick woman we read of in the fifth chapter of Mark. She too was a battered person terribly in need of compassion. She had not been physically abused, as far as we know; but without question, she had been battered socially, emotionally, and spiritually by the society in which she lived.

Oh, they didn't physically beat her or burn her with cigarettes, but emotionally, they shunned her; socially, they cast her out; spiritually, they labeled her "unclean." They told her that she was dirty and that everything and every person she touched she contaminated. They told her that God was angry with her and had set this misfortune on her because, in their minds, she had done some terrible thing to displease God. They laid guilt and shame on her by the bucketfuls, and they treated her with contempt.

Why? Simply because she was sick; simply because she had an unmentionable physical problem; simply because she'd had this flow of blood for twelve years. For twelve long years, her society had battered her. They wouldn't let her go to parties or to weddings or to the marketplace or to church. They wouldn't let her go anywhere she might touch another person. Think of what that would do to you emotionally and mentally and socially and spiritually. This woman was tremendously in need of a little compassion. Then one day, along came Jesus.

Jesus was on his way to see a little girl who was critically ill, when suddenly he was interrupted. As he was moving through the streets, people began to press in around him. *The New English Bible* puts it dramatically: "He could hardly breathe for the crowds" (Mark 5:24). The people were so excited to be near him that they were pushing and shoving and crowding in close to him.

In the crowd that day was this woman who had been hemorrhaging for twelve years. She wasn't even supposed to be in that crowd, but she was desperate. She slipped up behind Jesus, working her way through the crowd, and when no one was looking, she reached out, tentatively, fearfully, and touched the hem of his robe. Right then, the story tells us, her bleeding stopped. She thought she had gone unnoticed, so she dropped back and tried to lose herself in the huge crowd.

But then Jesus stopped, turned around, and said, "Who touched me?" The disciples were astonished by that question. Who touched you? What do you mean who touched you? Everybody's touching you. In this crowd, everybody's touching everybody. What kind of question is that? But Jesus knew that the disciples sometimes didn't know a push from a touch; and he knew that it was a special touch.

He began to look around. The woman had not expected to be found out. Timidly she stepped forward and told Jesus everything about her condition—how she had been bleeding for so many years and had tried everything, but nothing had helped. In fact, she had only gotten worse. She told Jesus that she had heard about him and his power to heal, and that she believed that if she could just touch his clothing, she could be made well; and it had worked! The bleeding had stopped. Jesus' heart went out to her, and he spoke to her tenderly: "Daughter, your faith has made you well; go in peace, and be healed of your disease" (Mark 5:34).

In this fascinating story we not only see the compassionate spirit of Jesus, but we also discover some of the key characteristics of compassion—very special qualities that we, as followers of Christ, need to let God cultivate in our own lives. Let's take a look at a few of these.

COMPASSION IS SELF-GIVING

One of the really beautiful moments in this story is found in the verse that tells us that Jesus felt that "power had gone forth from him" (Mark 5:30). This says to us that you can't help other people apathetically or half-heartedly; you have to give something of yourself.

A young, orphaned boy had been taken in by his grandmother. One night, their house caught fire. The grandmother tried to rescue the little boy, who was asleep upstairs, but she was overcome by smoke and lost her life in the disaster. As the house blazed, a crowd gathered. They could hear the little boy crying for help, but everyone seemed helpless in the confusion of the fire.

Then, all at once, a stranger rushed out of the crowd and climbed up a metal pipe that stretched past an upstairs window. The pipe was extremely hot, but the man ignored the pain. He went in the window, and in moments he reappeared with the boy in his arms. The crowd cheered loudly. The stranger climbed back down the hot pipe as the boy desperately clung to his neck.

Weeks later, a public hearing was held in the town hall to determine who should have custody of the little boy. Each person who wanted to adopt the child was given opportunity to speak. The first person, a farmer, said that he had a large farm where the boy could play outdoors. The second person, a teacher, said that her house had a large library where the boy could read and learn. After many others had spoken, the town's richest citizen suggested that because of his great wealth, he could offer the boy all of the other things mentioned, as well as many other opportunities that only wealth such as his could afford.

The group leader asked whether anyone else had anything to say. In the back of the hall, a stranger—who had quietly come in without being noticed—rose to his feet and began slowly walking toward the front of the room. It was obvious from his grim countenance that he had suffered much pain and anguish. As the man reached the front of the room and stood before the little boy, he said nothing, but slowly took his hands from his pockets; everyone present was shocked to see that his hands were scarred very badly.

Suddenly, the little boy cried out with surprise as he recognized the stranger standing before him: It was his own rescuer, the man who had saved his life! The scars on his hands were the burns he had received from climbing the hot metal pipe. With tears of joy and happiness, the boy fell into the open arms of the man, a stranger no longer. One by one the crowd departed—the farmer, the teacher, the rich man—until none were left but the little boy and the compassionate stranger, his new guardian, whose scarred hands had said more than words ever could.

Compassion is self-giving. As Christians, we should know that better than anybody because we serve one whose hands were scarred for us.

COMPASSION IS GRACIOUS

One of the most radiant qualities we see in Jesus is his graciousness. Notice how tender and gentle and loving Jesus is with this woman who touched the hem of his robe. He doesn't question whether she should be in the crowd. He doesn't fuss at her for interrupting him. He doesn't critique her theology or her superstitions or her expectations. He doesn't rebuke her for seeing him as a sort of last resort. He doesn't chastise her for touching him. He doesn't see her as unclean. Rather, he gives her the most gracious reception possible. And although we know the healing came from him, he humbly gives her the credit: "Your faith has made you well" (Mark 5:34).

A woman named Jenny was on an airplane one day. She had been busy going over some materials for the business meeting she would attend later that night. Suddenly, she realized it was lunchtime. The flight attendants were bringing out the food. She didn't really care for airline food, but she decided to try it. She was disappointed. The food tasted bland and stale, and her coffee was bitter. She sat there feeling sorry for herself and wishing for a better meal.

That's when she noticed the young man just across the aisle from her. He was in his early twenties, and he looked so pitiful and helpless. He obviously had been in an accident, for he was wearing a body cast from his waist to his neck. His arms and hands, covered with the hard cast, were immobile and useless. The flight attendant had put a tray of food in front of him, but there was no way he could feed himself. He just sat there looking at his food.

"Is the flight attendant going to help you eat?" Jenny asked him.

"I don't know," he answered. Jenny looked back and saw that they were busy serving the other passengers. Jenny asked if she might help him. He smiled and said, "That would be great. I'm really hungry." Jenny moved over to help him. It was awkward and embarrassing at first. Feeding another person is a very intimate thing to do. But soon it felt comfortable for both of them.

As he ate, he told Jenny about his accident. His name was Tom. He had been injured skiing while on spring break from college. Their spirits blended; it was a beautiful moment. When Tom had finished his meal, Jenny went back to hers, thinking that this meal was going to taste even worse than before because now it would be not only stale and bland but also cold.

Surprisingly, she was amazed: The food tasted absolutely delicious now! It tasted like something she had experienced before. The food that had been stale and the coffee that had been bitter now tasted wonderful. Why? They tasted like the bread and wine of the Lord's Supper. Jenny smiled across the aisle toward Tom because she knew that together they had just experienced Holy Communion.

That's the way it works. Anytime we reach out to others in the gracious spirit of Christ, there is Holy Communion. Compassion is both self-giving and gracious.

COMPASSION IS ACTIVE

Hal Luccock tells us that Eugene Ormandy once dislocated his shoulder while conducting the Philadelphia orchestra. What were they playing? Stravinsky, perhaps, but whatever it was, he was giving his all to it. Luccock then asked himself, "Have I ever dislocated anything, even a necktie?" (*Illustrations Unlimited*, p. 501). How about you? Have you ever done anything with that kind of zeal, energy, enthusiasm, or passion? That's what compassion is. It's energetic, enthusiastic, active love!

Have you ever wondered why Jesus called attention to the hemorrhaging woman? Why didn't he just let her slip away? Because by bringing her forward and announcing to the huge crowd that she was healed, he was saying to the people, "Look now! She's well! She's whole! She has been healed. God is not angry with her, so stop battering her. Let her reclaim her place in the community. Widen the circle and let her in."

You see, he had healed her physically. Now, he was actively healing her socially and spiritually. Jesus was the perfect picture of compassion because he was always anxious to love, eager to help, and quick to act. Real compassion is always self-giving and always gracious and always active, because, to paraphrase the late Oscar Hammerstein:

> A bell is not a bell till you ring it.
> A song is not a song till you sing it.
> Love is not put into your heart to stay—
> Love is only love when you give it away.

3
The Attitude of Confidence
Sailing Under Sealed Orders

WHEN HE ENTERED CAPERNAUM, A CENTURION CAME *to him, appealing to him and saying, "Lord, my servant is lying at home paralyzed, in terrible distress." And he said to him, "I will come and cure him." The centurion answered, "Lord, I am not worthy to have you come under my roof; but only speak the word, and my servant will be healed. For I also am a man under authority, with soldiers under me; and I say to one, 'Go,' and he goes, and to another, 'Come,' and he comes, and to my slave, 'Do this,' and the slave does it." When Jesus heard him, he was amazed and said to those who followed him, "Truly I tell you, in no one in Israel have I found such faith."*

—Matthew 8:5-10

Do you know what it means to "sail under sealed orders"? Anyone who has been in the Navy knows what that means. A ship is in the dock—perhaps at midnight. The crew is ready to sail, but they are waiting for their orders. Suddenly, an envelope comes to the captain on the bridge of the ship. The envelope is sealed. The captain knows that inside the envelope are the crew's orders, the details of the ship's mission and destination. Stamped on the front of the envelope, however, are the words "sailing under sealed orders," and printed on the outside of the envelope are some coordinates of latitude and longitude—a place in the middle of the ocean to which they are to sail.

For the sake of military secrecy, the captain has been trained not to open the envelope until he gets to that spot in the middle of the ocean. So, the ship and crew set sail, knowing not where they go, but trusting headquarters. When the ship reaches those coordinates of latitude and longitude out there in the middle of the ocean, then the captain opens the envelope and discovers what their destination is and what their mission is.

In a sense, the Christian faith is like that. We don't receive all the information for our lives at once. We move along, placing our confidence in headquarters; we move forward with confidence in God. We "sail under sealed orders" until we get to that place where God says, "Okay, you've made it this far. Now here is your next move."

One of the most highly respected missionaries today is a devout and committed Christian woman named Virginia Law Shell. She talks about trusting God when she describes something that happened one dark night in a missionary settlement deep in the heart of the Congo:

Older men served as night sentries for our missionary homes. They swept our yards, heated our bath water, guarded our houses, and were most useful in carrying notes at night between homes. . . .

One night I heard a familiar cough. When I went to the door, I could just make out the figure of Papa Jean, [one of the most dedicated sentries], holding out a note. It was a dark, tropical night. No moon or stars were shining. There were no street lights on this isolated mission station. A small, six-inch kerosene lantern with a smoky chimney in Papa Jean's hand gave the only smattering of light.

Such a pitiful little light in such a dark night I thought. "That lamp doesn't give much light, does it, Papa?" I said to him.

"No, it doesn't," he answered. "But it shines as far as I can step."

How often I remember [Papa Jean]. I can learn to trust God for my future, for I have learned that His light does always shine as far as I can step.

(Virginia Law Shell in *Good News* magazine, July/August 1990, p. 36, quoting from her book *As Far as I Can Step*)

Taking our best step forward and then having confidence in God to give us more light as we move along—that is a basic tenet of the Christian faith. This is the kind of confident faith demonstrated by the centurion who asks Jesus to heal his servant. When Jesus agrees to go and heal the servant, the centurion replies, "Lord, I am not worthy to have you come under my roof; but only speak the word, and my servant will be healed" (Matthew 8:8). A couple of verses later we read that Jesus is amazed by this and says to those who are following him, "Truly I tell you, in no one in Israel have I found such faith" (verse 10).

What confidence! What faith! What trust! The centurion knew without a doubt that Jesus would not let him down. He took the first step by asking Jesus for help, and he had confidence that Jesus would take the next one. What does this say to us today? Simply this: Let your number one priority be an intense desire to do the will of God. Accept God as the King of your life; then everything will fall in place for you. In other words, do your best now, in the present, and put your confidence in God for the future.

Let me bring this closer to home by lifting up three great resources that we, as Christians, can have confidence in.

WE CAN HAVE CONFIDENCE IN THE BIBLE

The Bible is the place to begin. John Wesley often referred to himself as "a man of the book." "At any price," he said, "give me that book." John Wesley said that many years ago, but it is still good advice.

Dr. William Willimon, Dean of the Chapel at Duke University, was visiting with a college student who was a member of one of the dormitory Bible-study groups on campus. The young man was telling Willimon about the group, and then he said, "You know, I've never been in a Bible-study group before. I never felt the need of it back in Des Moines."

"Why here?" Willimon asked him.

The student replied, "Dean, do you have any idea how difficult it is to be a sophomore and a Christian at the same time?"

That was a smart young man. He knew that he needed help, and he wisely turned to the Bible for direction and comfort and strength. He has confidence in the Bible.

Think about it like this. If somehow we were able to bring together the brightest minds of all time—psychologists, professors, theologians, lawyers, judges, scientists, doctors, and historians—and ask them to write a basic handbook for living a sane, meaningful, and productive life, a handbook that would be both profound and practical and would give straightforward instructions for zestful living, and if we put all their thoughts together and refined them and edited them down to a series of basic principles for living, we would discover that such a handbook had already been written many years ago: the Bible! And the efforts of these brilliant people would pale in comparison to what we already have in the Scriptures.

The point is this: "It's in the Book!" We've had it all

along. For nearly two thousand years, we have held in our hands the key to life—the instruction manual, the answer to the world's restless yearnings, the Word of God. Now, please don't misunderstand me. I am not suggesting that we can master the Bible in five minutes or in three easy lessons. I am not suggesting that finding life's answers in the Bible is as easy as thumbing through the answer pages in the back of a math book. No! Not at all. If we are to discover the great truths of the Scriptures, then we need to know how to study the Bible.

A minister friend of mine has a helpful suggestion. He tells about the time when he was a senior in college in Georgia. He was deeply in love and engaged to be married to a young woman who also was a senior in college, but who attended a school about 120 miles away. They wrote to each other every day. He tells how he would go to the campus post office every day and open box number four, pull out the regular letter from his fiancée, and immediately tear it open and read every word. Then he would close the box, pick up his things, and head across the campus to his dorm. On the way, he would read the letter a second time, oblivious to anyone else around. When he got to his room, he would close the door, sit down on the edge of his bed, and read the letter a third time, savoring every word. Finally, when he got up the next morning, he would read the letter a fourth time as the first act of devotion in the new day (William H. Hinson, *The Power of Holy Habits*, Abingdon Press, 1991; pages 80–81).

That's how it is when you are in love, and that is exactly how to read the Bible: like a letter from someone who truly and genuinely loves you.

One of the great gentlemen in the history of sports was a highly respected tennis champion named Arthur Ashe. Shortly before he died, he wrote his autobiography, which he entitled *Days of Grace* (Alfred A. Knopf, 1993). The closing chapter of that book is a personal letter to his young daughter, Camera. In the letter, Ashe shares with his daughter some observations about life and what he has learned, what he believes, and what he hopes for her after he dies. Here's what he wrote:

> Camera, have faith in God. Do not be tempted either by pleasures and material possessions, or by the claims of science and smart thinkers, into believing that religion is obsolete, that the worship of God is somehow beneath you. Spiritual nourishment is as important as physical nourishment, or intellectual nourishment. ... Do not beg God for favors. Instead, ask God for the wisdom to know what is right, what God wants done, and the will to do it. Know the Bible. Read the psalms and the Sermon on the Mount and everything else in that timeless book. You will find consolation in your darkest hours. You will find inscribed there the meaning of life and the way you should live. You will grow into a deeper understanding of life's meanings. (pp. 302–3)

You know what Ashe was saying to his daughter in that letter, don't you? He was saying, "Trust the Bible! There you will find God's way and God's Word. Don't let the world confuse you or deceive you or mislead you. Put your confidence in the Bible!"

That's our first great resource: We can have confidence in the Bible.

WE CAN HAVE CONFIDENCE IN THE CHURCH

I believe that we need to trust the mainline church now more than ever. Sadly, in recent years our world has, in large part, turned away from the church, mocked the church, ignored the church; and now that is coming back to haunt us in our nation. Recent polls have shown that more Americans are pessimistic than ever before: 71 percent of the people in our nation are dissatisfied with the way things are going in our country today; 62 percent think we are on the wrong track as a nation; 76 percent believe that our nation is in a moral and spiritual decline; and more Americans than ever before are worried and scared about crime, drugs, violence, and the lack of family values in our land.

Yet there is some good news. The truth is that this "cultural dissatisfaction" so many are feeling represents a rare opportunity for the Christian church. People are finally beginning to realize that secularism can't save us; that making more money and buying more things will not give us a sense of meaning or fulfillment or security or happiness; that a full stomach is not worth much, if the spirit is starving. The bleakness that so many are feeling today is driving people to raise fundamental questions about life, and that is a healthy sign.

A good friend sent me an article written by Charles Colson that speaks to this. The article was entitled "The Upside of Pessimism," and in it Colson said this:

> We have today a remarkable opportunity that Christians must seize quickly. Through the 1980s, anyone broaching moral issues in the public square was denounced as a bigot. . . . Yet today social decay is creating a deep hunger for moral truth.
>
> What can the church do? First, we need to make a credible case that Christianity can fill that hunger. . . . We don't have to bang anyone on the head with the Bible; we can simply present the facts. . . .
>
> Second, . . . we need to argue that Christianity is not just good for society; it is the truth . . . based on the One who is Truth. (*Christianity Today,* August 15, 1994)

Colson was saying, "Put your confidence in the church! There you will find God's way, God's Word, God's truth. Turn to the church. Support the church. Come to the church. Love the church. Listen to the church."

Let me say a word to the parents and grandparents who are reading these pages. What is the best thing we can do for our children? We love them. We love to give them gifts to show our love. What is the best gift we can give them? What is the most loving gift we can give them? A good answer to that question is the church. Talk about a gift that keeps on giving! Give them the church. Teach them the message of the church. Show them the holy habits of the church. Introduce them to the Christ of the church. Teach them that two of the greatest resources in which we can have confidence are the Bible and the church.

WE CAN HAVE CONFIDENCE IN GOD

Late one cold night in Washington, a pastor got a call from the bus station. The caller was a young man who had grown up in a church that the pastor had served some years before. This young man had gotten off the track. He had been experimenting with drugs, had lost touch with his family, and was out of work and hungry. Could this young man's former pastor give him some help on this cold, wintry night?

The pastor went to the bus station. When he saw the young man, he couldn't believe his eyes. He was filthy and tattered, emaciated in body and broken in spirit. The pastor brought him home. As the young man ate supper, the pastor asked him if he had ever asked God to help him.

"No," the young man answered, "but when I get myself together and start coming back to church, then I am going to ask Christ [God] to help me."

"My friend," said the pastor, "it will never happen that

way. If you think that you have to get yourself together on your own and then come to Christ, you will never do it. You're going to have to come to Christ as you are at this moment, and then he will give you the strength to start getting things together" (as quoted by John Claypool, "You Don't Have to Be Good to Come to Christ," *Preaching Today*'s Tape No. 83).

I don't know what your problems are, but I do know this: You can bring them to God and put your confidence in him, and he will help you. I don't know what your worries are, but I do know this: You can bring them to God and place your confidence in him, and he will help you. I don't know what your sins are, but I do know this: You can bring them to God and trust him, and he will help you. You see, we can have confidence in the Bible, we can have confidence in the church, and most of all, we can have confidence in God.

4

The Attitude of Determination

"Take Dead Aim!"

THEREFORE I TELL YOU, DO NOT WORRY ABOUT YOUR
*life, what you will eat or what you will drink, or about
your body, what you will wear. Is not life more than
food, and the body more than clothing? Look at the
birds of the air; they neither sow nor reap nor gather into
barns, and yet your heavenly Father feeds them.
Are you not of more value than they? And can any of
you by worrying add a single hour to your span of life?
And why do you worry about clothing? Consider the
lilies of the field, how they grow; they neither toil nor
spin, yet I tell you, even Solomon in all his glory was not
clothed like one of these. But if God so clothes the grass
of the field, which is alive today and tomorrow is thrown
into the oven, will he not much more clothe you—you of
little faith? Therefore do not worry, saying,
'What will we eat?' or 'What will we drink?' or 'What
will we wear?' For it is the Gentiles who strive for all
these things; and indeed your heavenly Father knows that
you need all these things. But strive first for the kingdom
of God and his righteousness, and all these things will be
given to you as well."*

—Matthew 6:25-33

It was the spring of 1995. Professional golfer Ben Crenshaw was in Augusta, Georgia, preparing for the Masters. He had won the green jacket in 1984, and he dreamed of winning it again. "Winning the Masters again. Nothing could be better," he had said. But then came the telephone call. Crenshaw's longtime friend and teacher, Harvey Penick, had died at the age of ninety. Crenshaw flew from Augusta to Austin for the funeral and served as one of the pallbearers.

Penick had been the resident pro at the Austin Country Club for fifty years, and he had taught some of the world's greatest golfers how to play the game. He took absolute pleasure in the triumphs of others, and his students loved to share their success with him. At his funeral, he was eulogized as a man who was "born in Austin and rarely left. The world came to him. The world fell in love with his goodness, his purity, his willingness to reach out and help people."

After the funeral, Crenshaw flew back to Augusta, determined to play his very best in the 1995 Masters as a loving tribute to his friend and longtime teacher. And, oh my, did he ever do that! Crenshaw won the Masters Tournament, and the sports world will long remember what happened when he made that final winning putt. He bent over at the waist on the 18th green and burst into tears! They were tears of joy over winning, tears of relief as he finished a week-long emotional roller-coaster ride, and tears of gratitude for all his beloved teacher had done for him and meant to him.

Back in the clubhouse, Crenshaw paid tribute to Penick when he said, "I had a fifteenth club in my bag, and it was Harvey." If asked what was the most important lesson he had learned from his teacher, he probably would have said, "Take dead aim! Take dead aim on every shot! Don't just swing and hope the ball will end up in the right place.

Don't just do it from time to time when you happen to think about it. Every time, every swing, every shot, take dead aim!" That's a pretty good stance for life too.

Another master teacher taught that lesson two thousand years ago. In the Sermon on the Mount, Jesus said it like this: "But strive first for the kingdom of God and his righteousness, and all these things will be given to you as well" (Matthew 6:33). In other words, Jesus was saying, "Put God first in your life! Take dead aim at God! Let everything you do be first aimed in the direction of serving God and God's kingdom, and everything else will fall in place for you. Not just every now and then, when you think about it, but every day, every decision, every moment: Aim your life toward God!" Let me break this down a bit by suggesting three things that can help us to do just that.

TAKE DEAD AIM AT HAVING
A STRONG RELATIONSHIP WITH GOD

There's a story that's been making the rounds about the time the Pope was scheduled to speak at the United Nations and his plane arrived quite late at Kennedy Airport. When the Pope ran out of the terminal and jumped into the waiting limousine, he told the driver, "Please hurry. I am to speak at the United Nations in just twenty minutes. Please step on it and get me there as fast as you can!"

The limousine driver said, "Sir, I'm really sorry, but I can't speed. I have already received two speeding tickets this year, and they told me that if I get another, I'll lose my license. I have a wife and three children at home to support, and I can't take that chance."

Hearing that, the Pope said, "I understand, but I have a solution. Let me drive! You get in the back and I'll drive and I'll get us there in a big hurry."

So they switched places. The driver took the back seat and the Pope took the wheel, and off they went, speeding through the streets of New York. As they sped down East River Drive, a young police officer pulled them over. The Pope showed him his international papers. The young police officer scratched his head and said, "Wait a minute. I need to call headquarters."

He went back to his patrol car, called his precinct, and got his captain on the phone. "Captain, I think I've messed up again," he said. "I stopped somebody really big."

"Oh no," said the captain. "Don't tell me you stopped the mayor again."

"No! It's not the mayor."

"Is it the governor?"

"No."

"Is it the senator?"

"No, bigger than that."

"You've got to be kidding. Who in the world have you stopped?"

"I don't know! I have no idea. But whoever he is, he's got the Pope driving for him!"

Now, that's a light treatment of a very serious subject, and here's the point: Let God be the driving force in your life! Let God take the driver's seat. Let God take the wheel and guide you and lead you and take you in the direction God wants you to go. Surrender yourself to God's will and God's service. Let God be your Lord and Master and Leader and Savior. Let God be the driving force in your life. Take dead aim at a strong relationship with God.

In the mid 1980s, the Minnesota Twins won their first American League championship in twenty-two years, and the city of Minneapolis went wild. They had a big party for the Twins at the Metrodome. Thousands of people were there, and the excitement was incredible. In the midst of this great celebration, with all of its pageantry and fanfare, a reporter stopped Greg Gagne, who was the shortstop for the Twins.

"Greg," he said, "this has got to be the greatest moment of your life!"

"Well," said Gagne, "this is a wonderful moment, and I'm enjoying this immensely; but in all honesty, the greatest moment of my life was that moment when I asked Jesus Christ to come into my heart."

Gagne was right. Everything else pales in comparison with that. So take dead aim at receiving Christ into your heart. Take dead aim at having a strong relationship with God.

TAKE DEAD AIM AT HAVING A STRONG RELATIONSHIP WITH YOUR FAMILY

It's incredibly important that we build strong families and strong moral values. Did you know that during the next hour, somewhere in America 138 children will run away from home, 76 children will be tragically abused, and 9 children will be arrested for drug offenses? This is what happens in our nation every hour of every day.

Mother's Day and the Festival of the Christian Home come around once each year in the month of May to remind us of how important it is to have solid homes and strong families. A Spanish proverb expresses it wonderfully like this: "An ounce of mother is worth a pound of clergy." A Middle Eastern proverb says this: "A child without a mother is like a door without a knob." One Mother's Day, a minister paid his mother this perfect tribute: "My mother practices what I preach."

The late author and humorist Erma Bombeck always had such poignant and beautiful things to say about mothers. One of my favorite articles was the one she entitled "Favorite Child." It includes these words:

> Every mother has a favorite child. She cannot help it. She is only human. . . . My favorite child is the one: who was too sick to eat the ice cream at his birthday party[; who] had measles at Christmas. . . .
> [who had] fever in the middle of the night . . .
> [who was] in my arms at the emergency ward. . . .
> [who] lost the money for his class ring. . . .
> [who messed up] the piano recital . . .
> [who] ran the wrong way with the football
> and [who] had his bike stolen because he was careless.
> All mothers have their favorite child. . . . The one who needs you [most] at the moment.

Sadly, family life in many quarters has fallen on hard times these days, and we've got to do something about that; we've got to turn that around. The fifth commandment says: "Honor your father and your mother, so that your days may be long in the land that the LORD your God is giving you" (Exodus 20:12). What does that mean? Simply this: When family life is strong, society endures and thrives. But when family life breaks down, it devastates society, because the home is the basic unit of society. Education begins at home. Self-awareness begins at home. Respect for law and order begins at home. Concern for others and love for God, the church, the Scriptures, and prayer—all of these should begin at home. A nation that destroys the family destroys itself.

Here's the challenge before us: Go and build strong Christian families. Take dead aim at a strong relationship with your family.

TAKE DEAD AIM AT HAVING
A STRONG RELATIONSHIP WITH YOUR CHURCH

In the early 1970s, a large commercial airplane was taxiing for takeoff at a major airport. The flight attendant was walking down the aisle to see that all passengers had their seatbelts securely fastened. She came upon one man whose seatbelt was carelessly thrown to one side. Instantly, she recognized the man. It was Muhammad Ali, who was at the time boxing's heavyweight champion of the world.

"Sir," she said with a smile, "you need to fasten your seatbelt."

Ali grinned at her and, as only he could, said, "Superman don't need no seatbelt!"

The flight attendant was quick with her response: "Honey, Superman don't need no airplane!"

We all need a spiritual seatbelt. We all need spiritual support. We all need the church. Sometimes we get out in the world and we think, "I'm Superman or I'm Superwoman, and I don't need the church!" But let me tell you something with all the feeling I have in my heart: You need the church! I need the church! We all need the church!

At the end of one wedding rehearsal dinner I attended, the handsome young groom stood up to thank everybody. His very first sentence moved everyone in the room to tears. Here's what he said: "If I lived thirty lifetimes, I could never repay my family for all they have done for me." Wasn't that a great statement? Well, that's exactly how I feel about the church: If I lived thirty lifetimes, I could never repay the church for all it has done for me. The church has given me a great family, a wonderful home, and a meaningful career. The church has given me a valuable education, a fulfilling social life, and so many wonderful friends. The church has given me support, encouragement, prayers, inspiration, direction, challenge, compassion, and comfort. The church has given me my ethics, my priorities, my attitude, my theology, my Bible. And the church has given me one more thing that only the church can give: Jesus Christ! There are many wonderful organizations and institutions in the world vying for our attention, our energy, and our resources; but the church is uniquely special because it exists for one purpose: to give us the love of Jesus Christ.

The message is clear: If you are to strive first for the kingdom of God, you must take dead aim at a strong relationship with God, a strong relationship with your family, and a strong relationship with your church. If you aim your life toward serving God and God's kingdom, everything else will fall in place for you!

5

The Attitude of Humility

"Not All of This Is Me"

WHEN THE DAY OF PENTECOST HAD COME, THEY *were all together in one place. And suddenly from heaven there came a sound like the rush of a violent wind, and it filled the entire house where they were sitting. Divided tongues, as of fire, appeared among them, and a tongue rested on each of them. All of them were filled with the Holy Spirit and began to speak in other languages, as the Spirit gave them ability.*

—Acts 2:1-4

A distinguished professor taught at the University of Chicago. Quite often, his preschool granddaughter would come to visit him at his office. She loved to reach up and hold his hand and walk around the campus with her grandfather.

One day, the man was carrying his granddaughter around on his shoulders. They met a friend who had seen the little girl just the week before. The friend looked up at the little girl riding on her grandfather's shoulders and, with a smile on his face and a twinkle in his eyes, said to her, "My goodness! Look at you! Look at how much you've grown since I saw you last week!"

The little girl replied, "Not all of this is me."

Of course, what she meant was, "I'm not really this tall. I'm not really this big. I'm riding on somebody else's shoulders." I like that story, because that sentiment so powerfully represents how I feel every single day. I go through life riding on the shoulders of others. I go through life riding on the shoulders of my family, my teachers, my mentors, my church, my staff. In addition, I go through life riding on the shoulders of the great Christians of history and the great people of faith who have gone before me in my own life. And as great as all that is, there is something better, something more important: I go through life carried on the shoulders of God and the Holy Spirit. You see, "not all of this is me."

Imagine that we could somehow get into a time machine, go back in history to the Day of Pentecost, and experience firsthand that incredible spiritual happening; and afterward we would go to Simon Peter and say to him, "Wow! What you did today was absolutely amazing! You stood and preached with astonishing courage and conviction, and your sermon was so powerful, so moving, that three thousand people came forward to join the church. Oh, Simon Peter, you were marvelous, fantastic! What a great witness! What a great sermon you preached!"

We know what Simon Peter would say, don't we? Of course we do! He would say, "Not all of this is me. Very little of this is me. It's the work of God. I was merely the instrument of God's Holy Spirit. I was riding on the shoulders of God's Holy Spirit."

Now imagine that we could get back in that time machine, fast-forward a few years, and find those early Christians who worked so hard to get the church going. Then we would say to Paul and Peter and James and John and Andrew and Barnabas and Priscilla and Aquila and Timothy: "Wow! What a great job you've done! Against all odds—against dangerous, life-threatening, frightening persecution—you have started so many churches in so many places. What an amazing accomplishment! How did you do it? How did you find the courage and energy and strength to do all that you've done?"

We know what those early Christian leaders would say, don't we? Of course we do! They would say, "Not all of this is us! Very little of this is us. It's the work of God. We're merely the instruments of God's Holy Spirit. We've been riding on the shoulders of God's Holy Spirit."

All of us should be able to relate to this, because the truth is that we all are riding on the shoulders of others. All of us are carried on the shoulders of our families, our friends, our colleagues, our church, and most important, our God. Whenever we do something that is good; whenever we strike a blow for justice; whenever we express faith, hope, and love; whenever we say a kind word or perform a compassionate deed; whenever we exhibit courage, confidence, or integrity; whenever we live in the Spirit of Jesus Christ, not all of that is us.

Actually, very little of that is us. When we stand tall for what is right, when we live out the Christian lifestyle, we are merely the instruments of the Holy Spirit. Let me bring this into focus by exploring three things that the Holy Spirit enables us to do.

THE HOLY SPIRIT ENABLES US TO FORGIVE

If we are able to forgive, it is simply because "not all of this is us." If someone has done you wrong and you are trying to find the strength to forgive all by yourself, all on your own, you are not going to be able to do it. It is the Holy Spirit within us that enables us to forgive. It is not our usual nature or immediate inclination to forgive.

When someone hurts us, we want vengeance! We want

to "get 'em back." We want to fight and show them a thing or two! That's our preferred reaction—until we open our hearts to the Holy Spirit. It is God's Holy Spirit who enables us to forgive. Better put, when we forgive, it's not really us; it is the gracious Holy Spirit of God forgiving through us.

In his books and newspaper columns, Lewis Grizzard often wrote about growing up in Georgia. One of my favorites was a column in which he told about standing outside his home church in Moreland, Georgia, and reminiscing about growing up in that little Methodist church that was so dear to his childhood. Grizzard fondly recalled going to Sunday school and to hear the preaching, though his church was small and had to share its preacher with a neighboring church. He also remembered being a part of the United Methodist Youth Fellowship, and one particularly remarkable event at one of those meetings. Two brothers, the town bullies, had broken into a store. As punishment, they had been ordered to attend Methodist Youth Fellowship meetings for six months:

> First night they were there, they beat up two fifth-graders and threw a Cokesbury Hymnal at the lady who met with us and always brought cookies. She ducked in time and then looked them squarely in their devilish eyes. Then soft as the angel she was, she said, "I don't approve of what you boys did here tonight, and neither does Jesus. But if he can forgive you, I guess I'll have to." She handed them a plate of cookies.
>
> And the last I heard, both [those boys grew up, and they're husbands and fathers] with steady jobs and rarely miss a Sunday [at church]. That was the first miracle I ever saw.

That was the miracle of forgiveness. If we could find that youth leader today and say to her, "How did you put up with those rowdy boys?" she probably would say, "Wasn't me. Left to my own devices, I would've poured the fruit punch on their heads and called the sheriff. But the Spirit of Jesus was in me. It was the Holy Spirit within me that gave me the strength to forgive." In other words, she would say, "Not all of this is me."

It's true for all of us: Not all of this is us. We are riding on somebody else's shoulders. When we find the grace to forgive, it is simply because we are being carried by the presence and power of the Holy Spirit.

Don't miss this: If you are unable to forgive, if you are having great difficulty forgiving someone who has hurt you or disappointed you, it may be a spiritual "red flag." It may mean that you have drifted away from the Spirit of God, because the Holy Spirit enables us to forgive.

THE HOLY SPIRIT ENABLES US TO LOVE UNCONDITIONALLY

If we are able to love unconditionally, it is simply because "not all of this is us." It's easy to love those who are attractive to us. It's easy to love those who love us back. But unconditional love—now, that's something else. Love to all, freely given; love expecting nothing in return; love with no strings attached; love even to those who hurt us—only God's Holy Spirit can give us the strength to love like that. Only God's Holy Spirit can enable us to love like Jesus loved.

Some years ago, a young man from the United States traveled to South America to fulfill his lifelong dream. He had a mission heart, and all of his life he had prepared himself to go to Colombia so that he could translate the Bible into the native language there and share the good news of the Scriptures with the people. But after he had been there for some time, the young man was kidnapped by Colombian rebels, who took his life. Imagine how his family and loved ones back home must have felt at the senseless and brutal death of this fine, innocent young man.

A year later, in an act of tremendous Christian love and kindness, the people of the young man's home community in the U.S.—church and civic groups alike— raised money to make a charitable gift to the people in the Colombian state where the young man had been killed. His parents traveled to Colombia for the presentation of the gift. After the ceremony, someone asked them, "How could you do this? How could you reach out in love to these people after what happened to your son here?"

The young man's mother responded, "We are able to do this because God has taken the hatred from our hearts."

We come in love because we are Christians. We serve Him who said, "They'll know you are Christians by your love." If we are able to love unconditionally, it is because the Holy Spirit is within us.

THE HOLY SPIRIT ENABLES US TO BUILD THE CHURCH

If we are able to build the church, it is simply because "not all of this is us." Only the Holy Spirit can build a church. Only the Holy Spirit can empower the church. Only the Holy Spirit can sustain the church. A church without the Holy Spirit is no church at all.

Mr. Holland's Opus is a movie about a dedicated music teacher named Glenn Holland. At the beginning of his career, Mr. Holland dreams of becoming a famous composer. He dreams of living in Hollywood and writing theme songs for movies, but he never gets to do that. Instead, he spends his entire career working with young students at John F. Kennedy High School. With great tenderness, he works with a red-haired girl with pigtails, who wants to play the clarinet. No one believes in her, no one helps her, no one encourages her but Mr. Holland. With great compassion, he works with an African American student who wants to play the drums but has a terrible time finding the beat. With great patience, he works with a street-wise tough kid who has a lousy attitude and is down on the world. Mr. Holland helps them all, and hundreds more like them.

The conclusion of the film is classic. Mr. Holland retires, and as he cleans out his music room at the high school, he tells his wife and his son that he feels like such a failure. He never accomplished his dream. He never went to Hollywood. He never became a famous composer. With slumped shoulders, he heads out of the school, but then he hears a noise in the auditorium. He opens the door and sees that the auditorium is jam-packed with his former students. They give him a long, thunderous standing ovation. They have come back to express their love and appreciation to this wonderful man who gave so much of his life to them. Then, the little girl with the red pigtails goes to the microphone. She's all grown up now and, in fact, is governor of the state. She says, "Mr. Holland, we know that you never got to become the famous composer you dreamed of being, but don't you see? Your greatest composition is what you did with us, your students. Mr. Holland, look around you. We are your great opus! Mr. Holland, we are the music of your life!"

Our calling as a church is to be God's music to the world, singing the song of forgiveness, the song of love, and the song of the church's great faith. But we can't do that alone. The good news of the Christian faith is that we don't have to do it alone; God is with us. The Holy Spirit is our strength, our guide, our inspiration, our comfort, our teacher. The Holy Spirit enables us to forgive, to love unconditionally, and to build the church. As Christians, we can live daily in the attitude of humility because we know that it is the Holy Spirit who empowers us; it is the Holy Spirit who guides us; it is the Holy Spirit who holds us up. Not all of this is us. We are carried by the Spirit of God.

6
The Attitude of Perseverance
"Never Give Up!"

*A*S FOR ME, I AM ALREADY BEING POURED OUT AS A *libation, and the time of my departure has come. I have fought the good fight, I have finished the race, I have kept the faith. From now on there is reserved for me the crown of righteousness, which the Lord, the righteous judge, will give me on that day, and not only to me but also to all who have longed for his appearing.*

—2 Timothy 4:6-8

It was the summer of 1968, and the world had "Olympic Fever." World-class athletes from almost every nation had gathered in Mexico City for the Olympic games. Thousands of eager spectators were on hand, and millions more all around the globe were huddled in front of their television sets to take in the action and to experience the spectacle of the games.

One of the most moving moments in the history of the Olympics came on the day of the marathon. A large number of well-trained runners from most every continent gathered at the starting line. The gun sounded, and the twenty-six mile race was underway. It wound through the streets of Mexico City and concluded in the Olympic stadium. The stadium was filled to capacity, and millions more watched by television as the race was finished and the awards ceremony began.

The bronze medal was presented, followed by the silver, and finally the gold medal was draped around the neck of the winner. He stood there proudly, eyes glistening, as the national anthem of his country was played and the flag of his country was raised.

When the awards ceremony was over, people turned their attention to other events. Some time later, there was a murmur in the crowd as the people in the stands realized that the marathon was not over. A runner was still on the course. The other marathoners had finished over an hour ago. But here came this young man from the African nation of Tanzania, limping his way agonizingly toward the finish line. He was in great pain. You could see it in his face and in the awkward way he was forcing himself to keep on running.

He had been injured in a fall early in the race. Now his knees were bleeding, his leg muscles were cramping, and dehydration was setting in; yet he kept on running. He would not stop. He would not quit. Finally, painfully, he crossed the finish line and fell to the ground.

A television reporter later told the story of the runner's injury and his determination to run through the pain. Then the reporter said to him, "You were injured early. You were hurting badly. You knew you could not win the race. Why didn't you just give up? Why didn't you stop? Why didn't you just quit?"

He answered, "My country did not send me five thousand miles to start the marathon. They sent me here to finish the marathon."

There is a great Christian lesson in this story from Olympic history: Perseverance is so crucial. Determination is so essential. It is so important to finish what we start. It's not enough to make a good beginning. It's not enough to run well for part of the way. We must finish what we start. We must see it through, or it is all of no avail!

Some years ago, Dr. Harry Emerson Fosdick, in *Twelve Tests of Character*, said it well:

> A very serious test of human fiber is involved in the fact that there are so many good beginnings and poor endings. . . . Good starters and good stayers are not necessarily the same people. Ardor, excitement . . . the flare of good intentions— such forces [get us] going, but they do not enable [us] to carry on when the going is hard. That requires another kind of moral energy which evidently is not so common as the first. Plenty of people are equipped with efficient self-starters. They get away easily. They are off with a fleet eagerness . . . but they peter out; they soon stick in the sand or stall on a high hill. . . .
>
> In one of our Federal prisons today is a man who for fifty years with unblemished reputation lived a life of probity and honor in his community. Then, as a government servant, he went to France . . . and mishandled funds. Only that will be remembered about him. The half century of fine living is blotted out. He was not able to finish.
>
> (George H. Doran Co., 1923; pp. 199–200)

In recent years we have seen it close at hand in the sports world, in the religious arena, on the political scene: Highly regarded leaders have faltered and faded, unable to see it through, unable to finish what they started. Against this backdrop, it becomes even more meaningful to hear the apostle Paul say, "I have fought the good fight, I have finished the race, I have kept the faith" (2 Timothy 4:7). Against this backdrop, the last words of Jesus from the cross ring out even more powerfully: "I have done it. I have seen it through. It is finished!" All through life and in every field—especially in faith—we see the importance of this kind of determination and perseverance.

One of the most beloved and colorful sports personalities of our time was a man named Jim Valvano—"Jimmy V," as he was affectionately known to sports fans around the country. Valvano died on April 16, 1993, after a year-long battle with cancer. He was forty-seven years old. He will be remembered as a great basketball coach. His North Carolina State team won the national championship in 1983, upsetting that great Houston Cougar team that featured Hakeem Olajuwon and Clyde Drexler. Valvano also will be remembered as an outstanding TV analyst, an eloquent inspirational speaker, and a lovable, wise-cracking humorist. But most of all, he will be remembered for the courageous way he faced a debilitating illness.

A few weeks before he died, Valvano was honored on national television, and to that vast viewing audience, he said this:

Today, I fight a different battle. You see, I have trouble walking and I have trouble standing for a long period of time. Cancer has taken away a lot of my physical abilities. Cancer is attacking and destroying my body. But what cancer cannot touch is my mind, my heart and my soul. I have faith in God . . . and hope that things might get better for me. But even if they don't I promise you this. I will never ever give up. I will never ever quit. And if cancer gets me . . . then I'll just try my best to go to heaven and I'll try my best to be the best coach they've ever seen up there. [Then, pointing to his 1983 Championship team, he said,] I learned a great lesson from these guys; they amazed me! They did things I wasn't sure they could do because they absolutely refused to give up! That was the theme of our championship season: "Never ever give up!" That's the lesson I learned from them and that's the message I leave with you: "Never give up. Never ever give up!"

That's precisely what Paul is saying in his second letter to Timothy: never give up; see it through; finish the race. Let me highlight a few of the things you must never give up as you make your way through life.

NEVER GIVE UP ON YOUR COMMITMENT

A story is told about a young college student who went into a photography studio one day. He had a framed picture of his girlfriend and wanted the picture duplicated. This, of course, meant that the picture had to be taken out of the frame. In doing this, the studio owner noticed that there was an inscription on the back of the photograph. It read: "My dearest Tom. I love you with all my heart. I love you more and more each day. I will love you forever and ever. I am yours completely for all eternity." It was signed "Diane," and it had this post script: "P.S. If we ever break up, I want this picture back." Sounds like Diane wasn't that committed!

I once ran across a list of great people in history who made it to greatness because they absolutely refused to give up on their dream. They were totally committed, and even though they faced major discouragements early on, they would not quit. They persevered because they were committed.

For instance, did you know that after Fred Astaire's first screen test, the MGM testing director wrote this memo about him: "Can't act. Slightly bald. Can dance a little." And did you know that Beethoven's teacher said that he was hopeless as a composer, and Caruso's teacher said that he really didn't have a voice at all, and Thomas Edison's teacher said he was not smart enough to learn anything? Did you know that the editor of the *Kansas City Star* fired a young cartoonist named Walt Disney because he said Walt Disney couldn't draw and wasn't creative? Did you know that Albert Einstein couldn't speak until he was four years old and couldn't read until he was seven, and that his teacher described him as "mentally slow, unsociable and adrift forever in his foolish dreams"? Louis Pasteur ranked fifteenth out of twenty-two students in his chemistry class, and the noted sculptor Rodin failed three times trying to get into art school, prompting his father to call him an idiot. Leo Tolstoy, who wrote *War and Peace,* flunked out of college. They said he was unable to learn. And Winston Churchill not only failed sixth grade but also went through a lifetime of failures before he finally became the Prime Minister of England at the age of sixty-two (*Chicken Soup for the Soul;* pages 228–30).

This kind of unwavering commitment is essential in the Christian faith. We can't do it halfway. We can't be wishy-washy about it. We can't be lukewarm. Total, complete, unshakable commitment is required!

There will always be those who try to discourage you, to pull you down and draw you away from your faith commitment. "You can't do it," they will say. "It's not relevant," they will say. "It doesn't work," they will say. "Try this instead," they will say.

But let me tell you something with all the feeling I have in my heart: Don't you listen to that! Don't be taken in! Don't be put off or shaken by the world's discouraging words. Don't waver in your commitment to God! The only way you can fight the good fight and keep the faith and finish the race is through unflinching commitment. Never give up on your commitment.

NEVER GIVE UP ON LOVE

In this tough world in which we live, there are moments when it seems like hate and prejudice and hostility are ruling the day. When we hear about churches being set on fire and little children being shot down in drive-by shootings and innocent people being blown away by terrorists' bombs, it seems like hatred is winning. But I don't believe that for a minute, because I know that love is the most powerful thing in all the world. Jesus showed us that on a cross, and I believe it with all my heart. So don't give up on love. Don't quit on love. Don't throw in the towel on love. Put love first. Make love the theme of your life.

Of course, when it comes to love, it's not enough to talk a good game. Christian love is active.

In one of the "Peanuts" cartoons, Lucy, who has a big-time crush on Schroeder, comes to him one day while he is playing his little piano and says, "Guess what, Schroeder? If you don't stop playing that piano right now and show me that you love me, you know what I'm going to do? I'm going to hold my breath until I pass out!"

Schroeder looks up from his piano and says, "Breath-holding in children is an interesting phenomenon. It could indicate a metabolic disorder. A forty milligram dose of Vitamin B6 twice a day might be helpful. I think that's probably it. You need Vitamin B6. You might also consider eating more bananas, avocados and beef liver."

As Schroeder goes back to his piano, Lucy looks out at the reading audience and says, "I ask for love, and all I get is beef liver!"

Cartoonist Charles Schulz was probably trying to say something akin to what the apostle Paul said at the beginning of the Love Chapter: "If I speak in the tongues of mortals and of angels, but do not have love, I am a noisy gong or a clanging cymbal" (1 Corinthians 13:1). In other words, when it comes to love, high-sounding words are not enough. Christian love, by definition, is active good-will. It is sharing the sacrificial love of Christ with the world. So the point is clear: Don't ever give up on your commitment, and don't ever give up on love.

Never Give Up on Jesus

In our hectic world, we can so easily become the victims of what author Marshall McLuhan called "implosion"—all kinds of ideas and causes and philosophies "exploding in" on us, vying for our attention and energy and loyalty and resources. What do we believe in? Where do we put our weight down? What do we give our heart to? Whom can we trust?

Well, we have the answer. We've had it all along. We've had it for over two thousand years. It's in the Book—the Bible. Jesus Christ is the answer yesterday, today, and forever. So don't be taken in by all these exotic, high-sounding fads that come along screaming for our allegiance. Just give your heart and soul to Jesus!

At a Promise Keepers rally, one of the leaders did an interesting thing. There were 42,000 men present. The leader said to them, "On the count of three, I want you to shout out as loud as you can the name of the town where you live." The men shouted out a variety of names, and it sounded like the Tower of Babel. Then he asked them to shout out as loudly as they could the name of their religious denomination. Again, total chaos. Then he asked them to shout out as loudly as they could their favorite sport. Once more, complete confusion. Then he asked them on the count of three to shout out as loudly as they could the name of their Savior. In perfect unison, 42,000 men shouted out—as clear as a bell—the name of Jesus! What was that leader trying to show? Simply this: Some of us like football, and others like basketball or baseball. Some of us are Methodists, and some are Baptists or Catholics or Presbyterians. Some of us are from Houston, and others are from St. Louis or Boston or Oklahoma City or Seattle. But the one thing we share in common, the one thing that unites us, the One who saves us, is Jesus!

There's no doubt about it: If we are to be faithful, effective Christians, we must cultivate the attitude of perseverance. If you want to "finish the race," don't ever give up. Don't give up on your commitment, don't give up on love, and don't give up on Jesus!

7
The Attitude of Open-mindedness
"Hiding Under the Couch and Hissing at What's New"

*S*O IF ANYONE IS IN CHRIST, THERE IS A NEW CREATION: *everything old has passed away; see, everything has become new!*

—*2 Corinthians 5:17*

Kenneth Chalker describes an experience his family went through a few years ago when they adopted a forty-pound, eleven-month-old dog. The happy, outgoing dog quickly took up residence in their home along with their numerous other pets—"four red-bellied newts, a frog, several fish, a gerbil, a rabbit, and an obnoxious cat."

They named the dog Ebony. She was very affectionate and was quickly accepted by all the other pets who lived there. Well, nearly all. There was one exception—the obnoxious cat, who took great offense to Ebony. The cat felt that his territory had been invaded by this newcomer, and he didn't like that one bit. So, in protest, and in obvious resentment, the cat became sullen and hostile. He took up residence under the couch in the family room and refused to come out. The cat then lived out its life hidden under the couch, and when anyone came near, the cat would hiss and rake his angry claws at whatever was out there. Soon, all the members of the family had scratched ankles, and poor little Ebony had a scratched nose.

It was amazing to watch the friendly dog and the cantankerous cat encounter each other. Ebony, the dog, tried her best to be friendly. She would repeatedly come to the couch and try to entice the cat to come out and play. She would even lie down, inviting the cat to check her out and be friends. But the cat absolutely refused. The cat stayed under the couch, fur on end, hissing at everything that passed, especially Ebony. He would swing his hostile claws at everything and everyone who came near. The cat would not listen to reason, would not give ear to persuasion, would not respond to love, would not be open to new possibilities or new friendships, would not give Ebony a chance. The cat just stayed secluded under the couch, fur on end, and hissed angrily at the newcomer and everyone else! (Adapted from Kenneth Chalker's "Spitting from the Closet," *Abingdon Preacher's Annual 1994;* pp. 42–3.)

That story encapsulates one of the greatest problems in our world today, the sin of closed-mindedness. New lives come near; new ways, new ideas, new challenges, new opportunities to love and to be loved present themselves. And so often, our response is like that of the sullen cat. We hide under the couch and hiss and slap at what is new. This fearful reaction to new things is as old as the Bible itself.

For example, remember Jonah. Jonah hated the Ninevites. All his life, he had been taught to detest the Ninevites, and the very thought of reaching out to these foreigners with kindness was the farthest thing from his mind.

But then along came God, saying, "Jonah, I have a job for you. I want you to go and preach to the Ninevites.

I want you to be my missionary to the Ninevites. I want you to take the word of salvation to the Ninevites." Jonah could not believe his ears. He would rather be dead than associate with those people. So he tried to run away. Like that resentful cat, he went under the couch, and he hissed and scratched at this new idea.

And remember the rich young ruler. There was an emptiness in his life. He had it made, by our world's standards. He was rich, he was young, and he was successful—a leader, a ruler, a man with power and clout, and yet something was missing, and he knew it. Deep down inside, there was this void, this ache, this longing for something more, this hunger that was not being fed. And then the rich young ruler heard about Jesus and the great things he was doing for people. And he thought, Jesus is the answer, so he came one day to the Master for help.

But when Jesus called on him to make the leap of faith, to put everything else aside and follow him, the rich young ruler didn't like the sound of that newfangled approach, and "his countenance fell and he turned away sorrowful" (Mark 10:22, Revised Standard Version), which is just another way of saying that he, like that angry cat, ran under the couch, hissing and scratching at this new way of doing things.

And isn't this exactly what the Pharisees did to Jesus? They didn't like his new ideas. They didn't like his new approach. They didn't like his newfangled way of teaching. They didn't like the new thoughts he was putting into people's heads.

"All this talk about love and grace and mercy and forgiveness and salvation and new life will just confuse the people," they hissed. "And look at him—associating with tax collectors and sinners; eating with poor people; touching sick people. Why, the very idea! We never did it that way before!" They complained and griped and criticized and hissed. And eventually they became so sullen, so threatened, and so jealous of this newcomer that they attacked him with all the hostility they could muster.

All through the Bible we see it—the sin of the closed mind—and how dangerous and destructive it can be. And yet the truth is that most of us can relate to that jealous, cantankerous cat. So often we are tempted to be threatened by a new approach, suspicious of the newcomer, fearful of the new way. But then the Scriptures bring us up short. The Scriptures celebrate God's new ways of revealing himself and his truth. This is what the apostle Paul is talking about in his letter to the Corinthians. The Corinthians were enslaved and shackled by their old ways of doing things, so Paul said to them (and to us) these remarkable words: "So if anyone is in Christ, there is a new creation: everything old has passed away; see, everything has become new!" In other words, put those old habits aside. It's a new day! Celebrate the new life that is available to you through faith in Jesus Christ.

Let me make this clearer with three thoughts.

BEWARE OF HISSING AT NEW IDEAS

Sadly, for some people there is no pain like the pain of a new idea. They have their own little thought world, and they don't want anybody or anything to disturb it.

Some years ago, I read a news article about a birthday party for a man who was celebrating his one-hundredth birthday. A reporter who was there to cover the event said to the guest of honor, "I guess you have seen lots of changes in your one hundred years," to which the elderly man replied, "Sure have, Sonny, and I've been against every one of them."

Or do you remember the story about the woman who came home from a gift shop with a beautiful plaque: "Prayer Changes Things." She put it up over the fireplace in the den, and it looked great. A short time later, the woman went to the grocery story, and when she returned home, the plaque was missing.

"What happened to my plaque?" she asked her husband.

"I took it down," he replied.

"Took it down?" she exclaimed. "Why? Don't you believe in prayer?"

To which he said, "Of course I believe in prayer; it's *change* I can't stand!"

Back in the eighteenth century, there was a huge controversy in the church in America about church music. Up to that point, hymns had been sung by what was called "lining." Most people didn't have hymnals, and those who did had books with only the words (and no music notes). The song leader would sing one phrase alone, and then the congregation would repeat that phrase. Then the song leader would sing the next phrase and the congregation would repeat, and so on.

But then along came a new idea. "Hey!" someone said, "Let's teach people how to read music, how to sing notes and parts and harmonies." To some, it seemed like a great idea; to others, it was absolutely scandalous. Immediately, Christians were divided as to whether "the old way" or "the new way" was proper. The controversy became a heated one. Sermons were preached and tracts written advocating one side or the other. In 1712, a tract was written by the Reverend Thomas Symmes of Bradford, Massachusetts, who favored the new way of singing. In his tract, he published what he considered the ridiculous objections he had heard to the new way, a kind of eighteenth-century Top Ten List. Here are some of these objections:

1. It is a new way, an unknown tongue.
2. It is not so melodious as the usual way.
3. There are so many tunes that we shall never have done learning them.
4. The practice of music creates disturbances, and causes people to behave indecently and disorderly. . . .
6. [I love this one!] The names given to the notes (do, re, mi, etc.) are bawdy, yea blasphemous.
7. It is a needless way, since our fathers got to heaven without it.
8. It is a contrivance to get money. . . .
10. [Those who want this kind of music] are a company of young upstarts . . . and some of them are lewd and loose persons.

(from Robert Mitchell's *I Don't Like That Music*, Hope Publishing Co., 1992)

The point is obvious. Some folks just don't like change, and they will offer any excuse, no matter how unreasonable, to avoid it. Like that cantankerous cat, they run under the couch and hiss at any idea that passes by.

BEWARE OF HISSING AT NEW APPROACHES

Recently, I discovered a fascinating story about two monks who were walking together through the countryside. Both had taken the vow of silence and the vow of cleanliness, which meant they were not to speak to or touch anyone. Their journey brought them to a shallow stream, but the water was moving rapidly. As they prepared to cross the river, they noticed a woman stranded there on the bank's edge. She was obviously afraid of the water and just stood there, petrified and helpless.

One of the monks just ignored her and began to cross the river. However, the second monk saw the woman, sensed her fear, and his heart went out to her. He knew that the law of his religion told him not to speak to her and not to touch her, but he also knew that a higher law told him to love and help people. So he picked the woman up and gently and carefully carried her across the swollen waters. On the other side, he tenderly put her on solid ground. She thanked him profusely. He smiled and waved, and then caught up with the other monk.

The other monk was disgusted with him for helping the woman. The two monks walked along in silence for several miles, and the first monk became angrier and angrier with the second monk. How could he have done that? How could he have broken his vow of cleanliness to help that woman? Finally, the first monk could hold it no longer. In total frustration, he turned to his fellow monk and shouted, "How could you have done that? How could you have broken your vow like that? How could you have touched that unclean woman?"

"She was afraid. She needed help," replied the second monk.

"That's no excuse," said the first monk.

"You broke your vow!"

The second monk paused for a moment, and then answered, "Oh my good Brother, I dropped that woman off ten miles ago. Why are you still carrying her?"

There is a great message in that story, and it's the same message the apostle Paul was giving the Corinthians: A new day has come, a new approach has come in Christ, and it's the way of love. The law of love is the higher law. It supersedes all the other rules and regulations, so throw off the old way of resentment and retribution. Get rid of those things that weigh you down, because now you are a new creation in Christ, with a new approach: Everything old has passed away; see, everything has become new.

BEWARE OF HISSING AT NEW LIFE

An elderly woman had an older model car. She had not driven it much, had taken perfect care of the car, and it was in excellent condition. However, one day as she was driving to town, her car was struck by another motorist. She was not hurt, but her beloved car was totaled. The insurance company told her not to worry. It was not her fault, and after considering the car's age, they would send her a settlement on the damage.

When the check arrived, she was so disappointed, so unhappy with the low amount that she went immediately to her insurance agent.

"But ma'am," said the agent as he opened his desk drawer, "I have the little Blue Book right here. It says that's all your car is worth."

With that, she reached into her purse and said, "Well, I have a little black Book right here. It says, 'Thou shalt not steal!'" And she got a higher settlement!

If you want a higher settlement in life, don't settle for anything less than Jesus Christ and the new life he (and only he) can give you! In the pages of this little black Book, you can find him, and if you will come to him in faith, he will leap off those pages into your heart and give you new life. Let me ask you. Is there something in your life right now that's pulling you down? Some old habit? Some destructive attitude? Some secret sin? Do you need to make a new start? Well, Christ is the answer. He can help you. He can help you throw off the old and put on the new. He can make you a new creation. Don't hiss at that. Rather, accept him with open arms.

8
The Attitude of Joy
"Them That *Has* Does!"

R EJOICE IN THE LORD ALWAYS; AGAIN I WILL SAY, *Rejoice. Let your gentleness be known to everyone. The Lord is near. Do not worry about anything, but in everything by prayer and supplication with thanksgiving let your requests be made known to God. And the peace of God, which surpasses all understanding, will guard your hearts and your minds in Christ Jesus.*

—Philippians 4:4-7

Some years ago, a train stopped somewhere in southern Georgia to take on water for the engine. A man on the train saw a local old-timer leaning against the depot platform, and he yelled to him: "Anybody around here enjoy religion?"

The old-timer shuffled his feet and replied: "Them that *has* does!" (Thanks to retired Bishop Ernest Fitzgerald for this story.)

Now, wouldn't you like to find that fellow and shake his hand? He made a major accomplishment with his answer. He spoke four words and made four grammatical errors! Isn't that something? Four English mistakes in a four-word sentence! That takes talent!

However, it should be noted that though his English was terrible, his theology was terrific. Forget how he said it and remember what he said. The question was, "Does anybody around here enjoy religion?" His answer was, "Them that *has* does!" That translates as "Those who really have religion (the right kind of religion) are radiantly joyous people!" Real religion does not make us somber, sullen, and sad; rather, real Christian faith makes us happy, confident, and glad.

Unfortunately, a great host of people have not made this discovery. They do not think of faith as a source of joy. They are pious, but not happy. They are conscientious, but not radiant. They are dedicated, but not joyful. Their personalities are, for the most part, grim, serious, heavy, burdened. They scowl more than they smile.

I remember a story about a little boy who went to church one Sunday morning with his grandmother, whose approach to religion was stern and puritanical. When the little boy saw a friend and smiled at him, the grandmother slapped his hand and said in a stage whisper, "Quit that grinning! Don't smile like that in church!" How sad it is—indeed, how tragic—that some people see faith as a source of goodness but not as a source of gladness. How sad that some people see religion as a sensitizer of conscience but not as a fountain of happiness.

Do you know what a *spoonerism* is? A *spoonerism* is an accidental transposition of sounds, usually the initial sounds of two or more words. For example, if you mean to say "well-oiled bicycle" and it comes out "well-boiled icicle," that is a spoonerism. This kind of verbal blooper is named for the Reverend William A. Spooner, a professor at New College in Oxford some years ago. He was famous for such mistakes. One of the most noted of all the verbal mistakes attributed to Spooner was the one in which he meant to say, "The cheerful tidings of the gospel," but it came out as "the tearful chidings of the gospel."

In that spoonerism is encapsulated one of the saddest mistakes in the history of religion—the fact that some well-meaning religious people have forgotten that our Christian faith is "good news of great joy." They have lost touch with the "cheerful tidings of the gospel" and have chosen instead to come down hard and threatening with the "tearful chidings."

This is, of course, a great pity, because our world desperately needs Christian people who are radiant and happy, joyful and confident, people who (as Paul put it) "rejoice always!" If there is one thing that the Christian gospel offers us, it is joy. Not a silly giddiness, but a deep abiding joy that stays with us even in the darkest circumstances. Happiness, gladness, confidence, abundant living—these are certainly a part of Christ's legacy to us, his people. Remember how he said it: "I have said these things to you so that my joy may be in you, and that your joy may be complete" (John 15:11).

Have we forgotten that the word *gospel* literally means "good news" or "glad tidings"? Have we forgotten the word of the angel that first Christmas night? "Fear not," it said, "for, behold, I bring you good tidings of great joy, which shall be to all people" (Luke 2:10, King James Version). If we do not have this sense of joy, if we do not have this deep spirit of happiness, then we are missing something God wants to give us; we are missing something basic to the Christian faith. Reminisce with me a few moments about this, and we will find it together. Here's the first thought.

THE BIBLE IS A RADIANTLY JOYFUL BOOK

Goethe once charged that Christianity is a religion of sorrow, but you certainly don't get that impression from reading the Bible. There is much sadness between its covers, but the dominant theme of the Scriptures is the note of gladness and victory. There is "agony" here to be sure, but much more, there is "ecstasy."

There is Nehemiah saying, "The joy of the LORD is your strength" (8:10). Job, in the midst of his suffering, contends that God will "fill your mouth with laughter, and your lips with shouts of joy" (8:21). Then there are the psalms. On almost every page of the psalms, the joy and triumph of faith resounds: "In your presence [O LORD] is fullness of joy; in your right hand are pleasures forevermore" (16:11). "My soul shall be joyful in the LORD: it shall rejoice in his salvation" (35:9, KJV). "Let all those that put their trust in thee rejoice: let them ever shout for joy" (5:11, KJV). "I was glad when they said unto me, Let us go into the house of the LORD" (122:1, KJV). Or consider Isaiah, who writes, "I will greatly rejoice in the LORD, my soul shall be joyful in my God" (61:10, KJV).

And when you leave the Old Testament and enter the New Testament, the note of joy heightens. Some years ago, Harry Emerson Fosdick put it like this: "The New Testament is the most joyful book in the world. It opens with joy over the birth of Jesus; and it ends with a superb picture of a multitude which no man can number, singing Hallelujah Choruses. No matter where you open it, amid fortunate or discouraging circumstances, you always hear the note of joy. . . . There is enough tragedy in the New Testament to make it the saddest book in the world, and instead it is the joyfullest" (*The Manhood of the Master;* pages 11–12).

The Bible is, indeed, a radiantly joyful book. Here is a second thought.

JESUS WAS A RADIANTLY JOYFUL PERSON

Unfortunately, our Lord has too often been pictured with a sad face. Artists have almost exclusively portrayed him as the man of sorrows. This is unfortunate, because nothing could be more false to the character of Jesus than to picture him as sad and gloomy, all bleached out. To the contrary, everywhere he went, Jesus carried with him, and into the lives of others, an atmosphere of happiness.

Think about it. If Jesus had been somber and severe, children would not have loved him so. If Jesus had been sad and sullen, the crowds would not have run after him; they would have run away from him. If Jesus had been cynical and sorrowful, people would not have come to ask him about the keys to real living. No, Jesus was not a killjoy. He was, and I say it reverently, the life of the party. He was radiant. His faith was joyful and confident—so much so that it was attractive, and people flocked to him because they wanted what he had. Consider this evidence:

1. Twice when the Pharisees attacked Jesus, they were upset because he and his disciples were having such a good time.
2. Jesus has given us the most joyous idea of God that has ever been imagined. God loves us like children. He is a gracious, merciful Father.
3. Jesus' happiness was not dependent upon material possessions or outer circumstances. His gladness was deeper, rooted in a sense of mission and partnership with the Father.

The Bible is a radiantly joyful book. Jesus was a radiantly joyful person. Now, here is a third thought.

CHRISTIANITY IS A RADIANTLY JOYFUL FAITH

We see it in the apostle Paul, who, in prison and in ill health, was able to say, "Rejoice in the Lord always; again

I will say, Rejoice." We see it in Saint Francis of Assisi, whose happiness was so contagious that even the animals were attracted to him. We see it in the great New England preacher of an earlier day, Phillips Brooks. A Boston newspaper once printed this item: "The day was dark and gloomy, but Phillips Brooks walked down Newspaper Row and all was bright."

We see it in the great Austrian composer Franz Joseph Haydn. A friend once asked him why his church music was so full of gladness, and Haydn replied, "I cannot make it otherwise. I write according to the thoughts I feel; when I think upon my God, my heart is so full of joy that the notes dance and leap from my pen; and since God has given me a cheerful heart, I can do no other than serve Him with a cheerful spirit."

Joy is our heritage as Christians. It is our legacy. Faith in Christ can give us a genuine and deep happiness that enables us to rejoice always, no matter what our outer circumstances. This happiness is not a shallow, "bubbly" feeling, but a deep mood of inner serenity, inner stability, inner joy.

I saw a beautiful example of this. One of our young persons, who once led the youth Sunday worship service, was a junior in college. His name is Mark.

At school, Mark became ill. He had an excruciating headache and was so nauseated that his roommate had to drive him to the hospital. When he arrived, the doctor found that Mark had a brain tumor.

On a Friday morning, they started operating on Mark when you and I would have been having breakfast; they were still operating when you and I would have been eating dinner. Eleven hours of surgery! But when Mark began to hemorrhage at midnight, they had to go back and operate for three more hours. They operated on him all day, and again through most of the night.

A few days before the surgery, I talked to Mark three different times. He was upbeat, confident, and serene. I said, "Mark, you are so upbeat, and I'm so proud of you for the way you are facing this difficult situation."

He said, "Jim, I've been going to church all my life, and I believe what you taught us in church—that God doesn't give us anything more than we can handle. I'm ready, and I believe that God is with me."

The day after the surgery, I went down to see Mark in neurological intensive care. He had been through surgery all day and all night, and, of course, he was very weak. He was sedated, and his eyes were closed. I took his hand and said, "Mark, this is Jim Moore," and immediately he squeezed my hand and gave me a thumbs-up sign. We had a prayer, and all through the prayer, at just the right moments, he squeezed my hand with courage and confidence, and with great faith. When I was ready to leave, I patted his hand and told him to "hang in there," and one more time, he gave me the thumbs-up.

That's what it means to rejoice always. To be confident in the faith that God is with us in every circumstance of life; and if we are faithful to him, the victory in this life, or the next, or both, will be ours. Nothing can separate us from God and his love—not even death, if we have faith in him. That's the good news of our faith, and that's why we can rejoice always. One poet put it like this:

> I am not sure the earth is round
> Nor that the sky is really blue.
> The tale of why the apples fall
> May or may not be true.
> I do not know what makes the tides
> Nor what tomorrow's world may do,
> But I have certainty enough
> For I am sure of you.

Amelia Burr wrote those words in her poem "Certainty Enough" about a friend of hers, but they describe equally well our relationship with the greatest Friend of all. That's what it's all about. That is the source of our joy, and that is why we can rejoice always in every circumstance. Anybody around here enjoy religion? Them that *has* does!

9
The Attitude of Faith
The Necessary Ingredients

*N*OW AFTER JOHN WAS ARRESTED, JESUS CAME TO *Galilee, proclaiming the good news of God, and saying, "The time is fulfilled, and the kingdom of God has come near; repent, and believe in the good news." As Jesus passed along the Sea of Galilee, he saw Simon and his brother Andrew casting a net into the sea—for they were fishermen. And Jesus said to them, "Follow me and I will make you fish for people." And immediately they left their nets and followed him. As he went a little farther, he saw James son of Zebedee and his brother John, who were in their boat mending the nets. Immediately he called them; and they left their father Zebedee in the boat with the hired men, and followed him.*

—Mark 1:14-20

Have you heard about the elderly woman who called the bank one morning? She wanted to check on her accounts and ask about getting a better return on her money.

The bank officer listened very carefully, then asked, "Well, Mrs. Jones, are you interested in conversion or redemption?"

There was a long pause before Mrs. Jones said, "Is this the bank or the church?"

We can understand Mrs. Jones's confusion because in this complex world, we sometimes have trouble understanding all the words. So with that in mind, let's zero in on the word *faith*, and see whether we can figure out what it really means. We hear people say, Have faith! Keep the faith! Receive the faith! Learn the faith! Share the faith! Proclaim the faith! Live the faith! But what in the world does that mean?

Recently, I ran across a colorful story that underscores and outlines the ingredients of faith fairly well. It's an old story about a man who was walking across a desert. The man was dying of thirst. He desperately needed water. Imagine his relief and delight when he came upon a pump, right out in the middle of the desert. There was a baking-soda can tied to the handle of the pump, and inside the can was a note. The note read, "This pump is all right as of June 1932. I put a new sucker-washer into it, and it ought to last five years. But the washer dries out, and the pump has got to be primed. Under the white rock, I buried a bottle of water. It's out of the sun and all corked up. There's enough in it to prime the pump, but not if you drink some first. So pour about one-fourth of the water in and let her soak to wet the leather. Then pour in the rest, medium-fast, and pump like crazy. You'll get water. The well has never run dry. Have faith. When you get watered up, fill the bottle up again, and put it back like you found it for the next feller. (Signed) Desert Pete. P.S.: Don't go drinking up the water first! Prime the pump with it, and you'll get all the water you can hold."

Over the years, many books have been written on the subject of faith, many sermons have been eloquently preached, and many lectures have been delivered. But Desert Pete (with his marvelous note) has graphically described, in his homespun way, the basic principles and ingredients of the Christian faith. What are they? Trust, risk, and work. We trust the message of Christ; risk our lives for the cause of Christ; and work to help others, in the name and spirit of Christ.

Trust, risk, and work; we see those three key ingredients dramatically in Mark 1, as Jesus comes to the seashore and calls those first disciples. "Follow me," he says, "and I will make you fish for people." In other words, "Come join me, and we will fish together for the hearts and souls of people." And look at what those four fishermen did. Immediately, they threw down their nets and left their boats, and they followed him. Talk about trust and risk and work! They dropped everything and followed him.

The word *follow* is a powerful word in the Scriptures. The Greek word for *follow* in the New Testament is *akolutheo,* and it carries a strong meaning. It means obedience—the kind of obedience a soldier gives his commanding officer. It means commitment—the kind of commitment that is unflinching, unwavering, unshakable. It means love—the kind of love that is total, sacrificial, and complete. It means devotion—the kind of devotion that calls us to lay ourselves on the line for a great cause.

This is serious business. Jesus is giving the call to faith and discipleship. When Jesus says, "Follow me," he doesn't mean, "Let's walk around the corner together," or "Let's jog back to town together." He is playing for keeps! He is asking for our devotion, our trust, our service, our loyalty. He is asking for our lives—our hearts, our souls, our minds, our strength. He is calling us to be his disciples. He is asking us to trust in him, to risk for him, and to work for him. Trust, risk, and work—these are, without question, key ingredients in the Christian faith. Let's take a closer look at each of these.

89

THERE IS TRUST

About a hundred or so years ago, an elderly gentleman was traveling alone on a train in France. A much younger man, sitting next to him, watched the older man take out his Bible and begin to read. After a while, the younger man decided to strike up a conversation, and he asked, "What are you reading?"

The older man replied, "I am reading from the sixth chapter of John in the New Testament."

"What does it say?" the younger man asked.

"Oh, it's the story of the miracle of the loaves and fishes. The Gospel writer tells us about a vast crowd that had followed Jesus because of the signs he was performing for the sick, and how Jesus preached to the crowd until it was dark. They were hungry, and with only five barley loaves and a couple of dried fish, Jesus fed the entire crowd of 5,000. And the leftovers filled twelve baskets."

Scornfully and cynically, the younger man said, "Surely you don't believe that!"

But the older man answered, "Oh, yes I do."

To which the younger man said, "Well, I can see that you have been brainwashed by ancient superstitions. Not me! That could never happen to me because, you see, I am a scientist. The only thing I trust and believe in is what can be proven scientifically. The story you have read defies the laws of science, and therefore I can't accept it. Give me facts, provable facts. As a man of science, I have no faith in miracles. But, of course, I can't expect you to understand that."

At that point, the train began to slow down. "Here is my station," said the young man as he rose from his seat. "It was nice talking to you, Mr.— Oh, I'm sorry, I didn't get your name." With that, the older man reached into his pocket and pulled out his business card. He handed it to the younger man. The younger man looked at it. Imagine

90

his surprise; the name on the card was Louis Pasteur! Louis Pasteur, of course, was one of the great scientists of all time, but he knew that the scientific method (valuable as it is) is not the only road to truth.

The real truth is that the best things in life cannot be proved in a scientific laboratory—love, courage, integrity, honesty, morality, perseverance, compassion, kindness, commitment, faith—you can't put those great things into a test tube, but we know how incredibly important they are. And we know how dramatically they were proclaimed in the life and death and resurrection of our Lord and Savior Jesus Christ. Faith is, first of all, the capacity to trust, to trust beyond what we can see and touch, to trust the message, to trust the call, to trust the church, to trust our God.

Recently I talked to a friend who has a terminal illness. She probably will not be here this time next year, but listen to what she said to me: "Jim, it's okay. I have had a good life, and now it's about over. I'm not afraid, because I trust God. I believe what we sing in our hymns and preach from our pulpits. God has been powerfully with me in this life, and I know he will be with me in the next."

Let me ask you. Do you have that kind of faith? Is your faith that strong? Can you trust in God like that? The first ingredient of faith is trust.

THERE IS RISK

A Middle Eastern chieftain tells the story about a spy who was captured and then sentenced to death by a general in the Persian army. This Persian general had a strange custom. He would give condemned criminals a choice between the firing squad and the big, black door. As the moment for execution drew near, the spy was brought before the Persian general, who asked, "What will it be: the firing squad or the big, black door?" The

91

condemned spy hesitated for a long time. It was a difficult decision, but eventually he chose the firing squad. Moments later, shots rang out, confirming the execution.

The general turned to his assistant and said, "Isn't that something? They always prefer the known way to the unknown. It is so characteristic of people to be afraid of the undefined. Yet, we gave him a choice."

"What lies beyond the big, black door?" asked the assistant.

"Freedom," the general replied, "but over the years, only a very few have been brave enough to take it."

This story graphically reminds us of how difficult it is to take a risk, to make the leap of faith. There is always the temptation to stay with the familiar, to stay with the known, to stay with the comfortable. When Jesus came to the seashore and said to Simon and Andrew and James and John, "Follow me," it would have been a lot easier for those four fishermen to stay with their boats. But look what they would have missed! They made the leap of faith, they took the risk, they dropped their familiar nets and followed him. And with him, they turned the world upside down.

All through the Bible, we see it: The great people of faith were people who trusted God and took a risk. They went out into the unknown, confident that God would go with them and see them through. Noah, Abraham, Joseph, Moses, Ruth, David, Mary, Paul, and many, many others like them trusted God and took the risk. Let me ask you: Will you take a risk? Will you really step out and follow Christ? Will you give your life to him, heart and soul and mind and strength? Two of the main ingredients of faith are trust and risk.

THERE IS WORK

The first thing Jesus did was to put those four fisher-men to work. "Follow me and I will make you fish for people," he said. In other words, a call to discipleship is a call to service, to work, to action.

Homer and Emmy Lou were courting on the front porch swing. Now, Homer was very much in love with his beautiful Emmy Lou. However, he was shy and often had difficulty mustering up the courage to express his love. Aware of this inability, he tried to express his affection with flowery words: "Emmy Lou, if I had a thousand eyes, they would all be looking at you." "Emmy Lou, if I had a thousand arms, they would all be hugging you." "Emmy Lou, if I had a thousand lips, they would all be kissing you."

Emmy Lou looked at Homer and replied, "Homer, stop complaining about what you don't have and start using what you do have."

The point is clear: Talking a good game is not enough. Just going through the rituals, just saying the creeds, just singing the hymns, just preaching the sermon, is not enough. We are called to practice what we preach. We are called to live our faith daily. We are called to be servants. We are called to be fishers of people. Only when our creeds become deeds are they worth anything. Only when our faith becomes active and goes to work is it worth much.

What does it mean to have faith? It means to trust, to risk, and to work; to trust the message of Christ; to risk our lives for the cause of Christ; and to work to help others in the Spirit of Christ.

10
The Attitude of Trust
"Let Him Play His Song"

WHILE APOLLOS WAS IN CORINTH, PAUL PASSED *through the interior regions and came to Ephesus, where he found some disciples. He said to them, "Did you receive the Holy Spirit when you became believers?" They replied, "No, we have not even heard that there is a Holy Spirit." Then he said, "Into what then were you baptized?" They answered, "Into John's baptism." Paul said, "John baptized with the baptism of repentance, telling the people to believe in the one who was to come after him, that is, in Jesus." On hearing this, they were baptized in the name of the Lord Jesus. When Paul had laid his hands on them, the Holy Spirit came upon them, and they spoke in tongues and prophesied—altogether there were about twelve of them.*

—Acts 19:1-7

A large stone cathedral in Europe was noted for its magnificent pipe organ. One Saturday afternoon, the church sexton was making one final check of the choir and organ loft high in the balcony at the back of the church. The sexton was startled to hear footsteps echoing up the stone stairway because he thought the cathedral doors were all securely locked and no one was around. He turned to see a man in slightly tattered traveling clothes coming toward him.

"Excuse me, sir," said the stranger. "I have come from quite a long distance to see the great organ in this cathedral. Would you mind opening the console so that I might get a closer look at it?"

The custodian at first refused, but the stranger seemed so eager and so insistent that he finally gave in.

"Do you think it would be all right if I just sat on the bench, for a brief moment?" asked the stranger.

"Absolutely not!" answered the custodian. "No way! Why, if the organist came in and found you sitting there, I would probably lose my job." But again the stranger was so persistent and so genuinely interested that the sexton gave in. "Okay, you can sit there, but please don't touch anything, and only for a moment."

The custodian noticed that the stranger seemed to be very much at home on the organ bench, so he was not completely surprised when the stranger asked if he could play the organ just a little bit.

"Oh, no!" said the custodian. "Absolutely not! It's out of the question. No one is allowed to play this instrument except the cathedral organist." The stranger's face fell. His deep disappointment was obvious.

Then the stranger said, "But I've come so far just to see and experience this organ. I know what I'm doing, and I promise that no harm will be done. I will handle this organ with great care and love." Finally, the sexton gave in, and he told the stranger he could play the instrument, but only a few notes, and then he would have to leave.

Overjoyed, the stranger pulled out some stops and began to play. Oh, my, did he play! Suddenly the cathedral was filled with the most beautiful music the custodian had ever heard in all his years in that place. The music seemed to lift him and carry him heavenward. It touched his heart like nothing before. In what seemed all too short a time, the dowdy stranger stopped playing, slid off the organ bench, thanked the custodian quickly, then turned and started down the stairs.

"Wait!" cried the custodian. "That was the most beautiful music I have ever heard in my life. It was absolutely incredible. Who are you, anyway?"

The stranger smiled and said, "My name is Mendelssohn, Felix Mendelssohn!" The custodian almost fainted! He had just heard Felix Mendelssohn play his cathedral's pipe organ, and he knew that Mendelssohn was one of the greatest organists and composers of the nineteenth century.

After Mendelssohn left, the custodian was alone in that magnificent cathedral, and he could still hear that incredible organ music ringing in his ears.

"Just think," he said softly, "I almost kept the master from playing his music in my cathedral!" (*Illustrations Unlimited*; pp. 71–2).

This is a parable for each of us, because we are so like that custodian. So often, we are tempted to say "no" to the Master. So often, we are anxious to hold Christ at arm's length. So often, we are fearful of letting our Lord come too close. So often, we are afraid to let the Spirit of God play his song in us. "No!" we say to the Master, "Don't get too close! Don't touch! Don't break into my routine! Don't intrude in my life! Keep your distance! I don't want to get too involved with you!"

In Acts 19, we see another graphic example of this. Empowered by the Holy Spirit, Paul has been traveling far and near, starting churches. He comes one day to the city of Ephesus and discovers some disciples there. He says to them, "Did you receive the Holy Spirit when you became believers?"

And—listen to this—they answer, "No, we have not even heard that there is a Holy Spirit." Then Paul tells them the story of Jesus and baptizes them in the name of Jesus. Then, the Scriptures tell us, "The Holy Spirit came upon them, and they spoke in tongues and prophesied." This is another way of saying that they had new power, new strength, new capabilities, new life, because the Holy Spirit had come into their hearts. They were nominal Christians before—Christians in name, before, but they had no real power until they had been touched by the Holy Spirit. Myra Brooks Welch's beloved poem "The Touch of the Master's Hand" expresses it well:

'Twas battered and scarred, and the auctioneer
Thought it scarcely worth his while
To waste much time on the old violin
But held it up with a smile.
"What am I bidden, good folks," he cried,
"Who'll start the bidding for me?"
"A dollar, a dollar"; then "Two! Only two?
Two dollars, who'll make it three?
Three dollars, once; three dollars, twice;
Going for three—" But no,
From the room, far back, a gray-haired man
Came forward and picked up the bow;
Then, wiping the dust from the old violin,
And tightening the loose strings,
He played a melody pure and sweet
As a caroling angel sings.

The music ceased, and the auctioneer,
With a voice that was quiet and low,
Said: "What am I bid for the old violin?"
And he held it up with the bow.
"A thousand dollars, and who'll make it two?
Two thousand! And who'll make it three?
Three thousand, once; three thousand, twice,

And going, and gone," said he.
The people cheered, but some of them cried,
"We do not quite understand
What changed its worth." Swift came the reply:
"The touch of a master's hand."

And many a [one] with life out of tune,
And battered and scarred with sin,
Is auctioned cheap to the thoughtless crowd,
Much like the old violin.
A "mess of pottage," a glass of wine;
A game—and he travels on.
He is "going" once, and "going" twice,
He's "going" and almost "gone."
But the Master comes, and the foolish crowd
Never can quite understand
The worth of a soul and the change that's wrought
By the touch of the Master's hand.

The point is clear: Welcome the Master into your life!
Trust him completely! Be open to the touch of the Master's hand! Receive the Spirit into your heart! Let him play his song in you! Now, let me be more specific with three thoughts. Are you ready? Here's the first one.

TRUST GOD TO PLAY HIS SONG OF FORGIVENESS IN YOU

On Saturday, June 8, 1996, there was an amazing story in the *Houston Chronicle*. It told about Stephanie Palmer, who for many years had had everything going for her. She was an attractive, socially active mother of three, who led a comfortable and peaceful life until December 19, 1993.

That day, a robber invaded her home. At gunpoint, he made Stephanie and her family lie face down on the floor while he ransacked the house. One of the children became understandably upset, and when Stephanie raised her head to calm her child, the robber shot her, blowing away the right side of her face. For four days in the hospital, she hovered between life and death. Since then, she has undergone more than twenty surgeries for her facial disfigurement and has had to feed herself through a straw. Her speech, vision, and hearing also have been affected by her injuries.

"My initial fear," she said, "was that my kids might be afraid of me. . . . But, I've overcome that, because it's really not what's on the outside, it's what's on the inside. My children are wonderful. They don't treat me any differently. My husband tells me how beautiful I am. . . . He knew the real me before this happened. I get stared at; I get laughed at. It's difficult, but God is with me, and I know that with God in charge, I'll do pretty good."

Now, here's the amazing part of this story. On Friday, June 7, 1996, the robber was convicted and sentenced to life imprisonment. Stephanie Palmer calmly walked to the witness stand to give her victim-impact statement. She looked at the man who had robbed her and shot her, and graciously she said, "I think there's only one thing left for me to say, and that's that I forgive you." Stephanie Palmer's spirit of forgiveness struck some as shocking, but those who know her weren't surprised at all.

Now, let me ask you. Where did she learn to forgive like that? Where did she get the strength to forgive like that? You know the answer, don't you? She got it from the Lord. She got it from her Master. She got it from his Holy Spirit. You know what I think? I think that if we went to Stephanie Palmer today and asked her, "Why did you forgive the man who did that awful thing to you?" she would say, "Because I'm a Christian; because I serve him who said, 'Love your enemies and pray for those who persecute you.' Because I follow the One who, even as he was being crucified, said from a cross, 'Father, forgive them, they know not what they do.' "

And, I think, she would add, "It's not really me. It's the Spirit of God in me, giving me the strength to do incredible things." Can you forgive like that? Is the Spirit of God powerfully in you, enabling you to forgive? That's the first thought: Trust God to play his song of forgiveness in you.

TRUST GOD TO PLAY HIS SONG OF CONFIDENCE IN YOU

Poise, power, courage, serenity, hope, blessed assurance—whatever you want to call it—it's the confidence that God is with us. There is amazing strength in believing that, trusting that, and having faith in God.

Back in the 1970s, there was a wonderful story that came out of the San Diego Chargers' football team history. These were the years when Dan Fouts was just beginning to rise to greatness as a pro quarterback. The Chargers also had a backup quarterback, named Bobby Douglas. In one of their games that year, the Chargers had a bad day. They were behind 14-0, with only two minutes left to play. In frustration, the coach pulled Dan Fouts out of the game and told Bobby Douglas to go in and finish.

Douglas was so excited to get in the game! He quickly strapped on his helmet and raced toward the huddle. But about three-fourths of the way onto the field, he stopped dead in his tracks. He looked at the scoreboard and saw that his team was behind 14-0, with less than two minutes left in the game. He turned around, ran back to the sidelines, and said to the coach, "Coach, do you want me to win the game? Or just tie it?"

That's the kind of confidence we can have as Christians. Not because of our strengths or ability or might, but because of God's powerful presence with us. Look at some of the different ways the Bible expresses that:

101

Ephesians 6:10: "Be strong in the Lord and in the strength of his power."

2 Timothy 2:1: "Be strong in the grace that is in Christ Jesus."

1 Peter 4:11: "Whoever serves must do so with the strength that God supplies."

Colossians 1:11: "May you be made strong with all the strength that comes from his glorious power."

And I love the way Dietrich Bonhoeffer put this. He said that we can be confident as Christians because "God will give us all the strength that we need in times of trial; but God never gives it to us in advance, lest we think the power comes from us and not from Him." So, we can trust God and let the Spirit of God play his song of forgiveness and his song of confidence in you.

TRUST GOD TO PLAY HIS SONG OF VICTORY IN YOU

Winston Churchill planned his own funeral, which took place in Saint Paul's Cathedral in London. Churchill included in the service many of the great and triumphant hymns of the church and many of the victorious passages of Scripture, but then came a surprise ending. Following his instructions, as soon as the benediction was concluded, a bugler positioned high up in the dome of the cathedral solemnly played "Taps"—"Now the day is over."

But then came the most dramatic turn. Churchill had directed that as soon as the bugler played the final note of "Taps," another bugler, on the other side of the dome, would begin to play "Reveille"—"It's time to get up! It's time to get up!" What was Churchill trying to say? Simply this: For Christians, the last note will not be "Taps"; it will be "Reveille"!

This is one of the greatest promises of the Bible—as Christians, nothing can defeat us, because God is with us. Nothing—not even death—can defeat us, because God gives us the victory! So trust God, and let him play his song. Let him play in you his song of forgiveness, his song of confidence, his song of victory.

11
The Attitude of Commitment

"Be Strong"

*Y*OU THEN, MY CHILD, BE STRONG IN THE GRACE THAT IS
*in Christ Jesus; and what you have heard from me
through many witnesses entrust to faithful people who
will be able to teach others as well. Share in suffering
like a good soldier of Christ Jesus. No one serving in the
army gets entangled in everyday affairs; the soldier's aim
is to please the enlisting officer. And in the case of an
athlete, no one is crowned without competing according
to the rules. It is the farmer who does the work who
ought to have the first share of the crops.
Think over what I say, for the Lord will give you
understanding in all things.*

—2 Timothy 2:1-7

A recent article on the sports page of the *Houston
Chronicle* made me cry. It brought tears to my eyes.
Maybe that's not so unusual these days. Those of us who
love Houston and who love sports felt like crying (or did)
when we read stories about the Oilers' move to Nashville
and the Astros' possible move to Virginia. Those of us
who love sports feel like crying when we read stories
about greed and corruption and selfishness and gambling

and drugs in the sports world. We want to cry when we read the constant barrage of news reports about bickering and fighting and lawsuits and lack of loyalty in sports.

Those of us who could not even imagine Stan Musial playing for anybody other than the Cardinals, or Earl Campbell wearing any other professional uniform than the Oiler Blue, or Calvin Murphy holding out for more money, do want to cry when we read stories about a twenty-four-year-old athlete's complaining and whining because he is only making three million dollars a year to play a game.

However, on October 13, 1995, I read a story on the sports page of the *Houston Chronicle* that made me cry a different kind of tears. It was written by Ed Fowler and was titled "A Sure Way to Spot Champ with Heart." The story is about Houston Rockets superstar basketball player Hakeem Olajuwon and his visit with nine-year-old David Segal. David had cancer, and he was dying. His last request was to meet Hakeem. The Make-a-Wish Foundation notified Hakeem, and he rushed to the hospital to see David. Here's how Ed Fowler described what happened that night:

> Often famous athletes are called upon to visit dying children, and often they fumble for parting words, as most of us would under the circumstances. Typically, a celebrity on his way out the door of the hospital room will babble, "I hope you feel better," or something equally banal.
>
> Hakeem Olajuwon did not.
>
> The Rockets center received word at the end of last November that the one and only wish of 9-year-old David Segal was to meet him. It was, in the terminology of Make-a-Wish Foundation workers, a "rush wish." In this case, that meant David's doctor had given them twenty-four hours to make it happen.
>
> The request went through the Rockets' front office to Olajuwon, who agreed immediately. The team was play-

ing Denver at The Summit that night. Club officials prepared a goody bag filled with memorabilia for the player to sign, and Olajuwon proceeded directly from the arena after the game to make the visit.

David, born in Houston, had been a basketball fan almost since birth. . . . He [had become] attached to the Rockets, and to Olajuwon in particular. David liked airplanes and "Sesame Street," and he liked to read, but following the Rockets was his passion. He watched them on television and attended several games, but he didn't get to go to The Summit as often as he would have liked.

Just as he reached the age at which he could appreciate watching a game in person, his father, Dr. Ian Segal, learned he had cancer. That illness diverted the family's energy from pursuits such as basketball until David's father died in August 1993.

On October 29, 1994 [at the age of nine], David was diagnosed with lung cancer. He died December 1, 1994.

As he lay in his hospital bed (in those final hours), a Make-a-Wish volunteer offered to do the utmost to grant his last request.

David wanted to meet Hakeem, and Hakeem wanted to meet David when he learned of his case. After the game with Denver, Olajuwon . . . followed volunteers to the hospital.

[David] had been moving in and out of consciousness, but he had prepared a list of questions for Olajuwon, some of them highly personal. Olajuwon sat on David's bed and answered each of them, signed the items in the bag and posed for pictures. [Finally,] seeing the youngster's exhaustion, Olajuwon rose to leave. His last words to David were, "Be strong."

Volunteers rushed out to get the pictures developed and returned in time to show them to David, generating one last weak smile. With his No. 34 cap at hand, David died a few hours later. A photo of him with Olajuwon was displayed at his funeral.

Olajuwon wasn't informed of David's death until after the Rockets' game the next night. At his request, the photos of his visit and the questions the youngster posed have not been released, but those who were there say Hakeem was moved.

Among them was Teri Andrepont, executive director of the Make-a-Wish chapter. "You know me," she says. "I don't care much about athletes and all your sports stuff, but this is what the heart of a champion is to me."

Sometimes the world is too tough, and sometimes life seems so unfair. And sometimes the only thing that can be said is what Hakeem Olajuwon said to nine-year-old David Segal on that dark November night—"Be strong!" Interestingly, that modern-day story reminds me of something in the Bible, something that happened some 2,000 years ago. This story too revolves around a seasoned veteran superstar who had the heart of a champion, giving advice and counsel to a young man facing a tough, harsh, and unfair world. The seasoned veteran in the Bible story was the apostle Paul, and the young man was Paul's young coworker, Timothy. And the message from Paul to Timothy was simply this: Be strong!

For more than fifteen years, Paul and Timothy had worked together, spreading the gospel of Jesus Christ and starting churches throughout Asia and Greece. But now Paul had been arrested and was in prison in Rome, facing death. And young Timothy was trying to lead the church through a time of terrible persecution. It took incredible courage and great commitment to be a Christian in those early days. They were attacked and reviled and slandered and falsely accused. Some were burned at the stake or fed to the lions—and those were the more kindly deaths.

William Barclay, in his commentary on *The Gospel of Matthew, Vol. 1*, gives this graphic description: "Nero wrapped the Christians in pitch and set them alight, and used them as living torches to light his gardens. He sewed them in the skins of wild animals and set his hunting dogs upon them to tear them to death. They were tortured on the rack; they were scraped with pincers; molten lead was poured hissing upon them.... These things are not pleasant to think about, but these are the things [you] had to be prepared for, if [you] took [your] stand with Christ" (Revised Edition, Westminster, 1975; p. 112).

And in that time of persecution, when the apostle Paul wrote to young Timothy, he said to him, "Be strong!" These were not just naive "Pollyanna" words that Paul was piously speaking into the air. As he spoke them, he was practicing what he was preaching. Paul was in prison in chains, facing martyrdom, when he wrote these words. And notice how he said it. He didn't just say, "Be strong." He said, "Be strong in the grace that is in Christ Jesus."

I like the way *The New English Bible* puts it: "Take strength from the grace of God which is ours in Christ Jesus" (verse 1). What does that mean? Simply this. If we are faithful in our commitment to Christ, nothing can defeat us. No persecution, no hardship, no disease, not even death can defeat us, because Christ has already given us the victory. It means that we can "be strong" because God is with us, and (come what may) ultimately God will win, and God wants to share that victory with you and with me. If the apostle Paul could speak to you and me today, what would he say to us? Let me suggest three things, and I'm sure you will think of others.

PAUL WOULD SAY, BE STRONG IN YOUR COMMITMENT TO CHRIST

Diane Komp tells of a father and mother and their two children. Ann and her husband were typical married boomers. Well-off financially, they had little time for church and very little time for each other. Their romance had faded, but neither wanted to give up their lifestyle. Besides, they adored their children, and T.J., their youngest son, was especially delightful.

The children were never taken to church, never sent to Sunday school, and the name of God was never mentioned in their home, but one day, unexpectedly, T.J. said, "Mama, I love you more than *anything* in the world, except God. And I love him a little bit more." Ann was most surprised, but she assured T.J. that it was all right. However, she kept wondering why he would speak of God like that. Two days later, T.J. was crossing a snow-covered creek and fell through the ice, tragically resulting in his death.

Ann remembers being so angry with God, but even as she lashed out in her grief and bitterness, she felt herself held in loving arms. Her world now in pieces, she remembered the Christmas gift T.J. had bought her that week. He had kept trying to give it to her before Christmas, but each time, she would laugh and tell him to put it away until Christmas Day. When Ann returned home after the accident, she hurried upstairs to T.J.'s room and opened the gift. Inside was a beautiful necklace with a cross.

That cross saved Ann's life. In the days that followed, it helped Ann to reach out to others, rather than becoming lost in her own anger and grief. Helping others helped her. That cross saved her life. It gave her the strength and courage to endure that difficult day and the hard months that followed. A gradual transformation took place in the lives of both Ann and her husband. They felt the presence of Christ in their midst, and together they worked to help others discover the strength that comes from Christ's presence.

They dedicated themselves to a new ministry—the mission of reaching out to other families who have lost children in tragic accidents—saying, "We've been through that and we want to help you get through it." To date, Ann and her husband have helped more than two hundred families work through that agonizing grief experience of suddenly losing a child. They call their effort T.J. Ministries, not only for their son, T.J., but also to emphasize how they have been able to deal with their loss and go on to help others, as they say, "Through Jesus" (Diane M. Komp, *A Window to Heaven: When Children See Life in Death*, Zondervan, 1992; pages 81–3).

Through Jesus, they have found the strength and courage to go on, to meet life with steady eyes and reach out to help others get through that hard valley of grief and pain. This is what the apostle Paul was saying to Timothy long ago, and it is what he is saying to you and me right now: "Be strong" in your commitment to Christ, and his strength will see you through. Whatever hardships or heartaches or persecutions or pains or troubles or temptations may come your way, don't waver—"Be strong" in your commitment to Christ.

PAUL WOULD SAY, BE STRONG IN YOUR COMMITMENT TO COMPASSION

"Be strong" in your commitment to love! Put love first! Let the compassion of Christ flow into your heart and out to others. Dedicate yourself to the spirit of love.

Some years ago, a California realtor took the famous comedian Groucho Marx to see a palatial ocean-front estate that was for sale. The salesman drove Groucho up the mile-long, beautifully landscaped drive. He escorted him through the house, the stables, the gardens, and the kennels, showing off the exquisite features of this dream palace by the sea. Groucho plodded along after him, nodding from time to time, apparently very impressed with the incredible castle-estate.

Finally they went out on the flagstone terrace, and the salesman, warming to the occasion and moving in to make the sale, waved proudly toward the broad expanse of the gorgeous blue waters of the Pacific and said, "Now, just look at that! What do you think?"

"I don't care for it," Groucho replied, and then, as only Groucho could, he pointed toward the gorgeous view and said: "Take away the ocean and what have you got!" (Thanks to Rod Wilmoth for this story.)

That story is a parable for us. We may look good outwardly. We may know the Bible from cover to cover. We may be respectable people. We may be steeped in church history. We may be well-versed in theology. We may know hundreds of sacred hymns by heart. We may even be able to speak in tongues. But take away love, and what have we got? As the apostle Paul put it so powerfully in the Love Chapter (1 Corinthians 13), if we don't have love, we have nothing and we are nothing. Jesus called it the key sign of discipleship, so the message is clear: Be strong in your commitment to Christ, and be strong in your commitment to love and compassion.

PAUL WOULD SAY, BE STRONG IN YOUR COMMITMENT TO THE CHURCH

This is really what the apostle Paul was saying to Timothy in that letter long ago. Keep the church going! Keep the church alive and well! Don't waver! Don't weaken! Don't quit! Come what may, stay faithful and trust God to make it right! Be strong in your commitment to the church.

Let me ask you: How strong is your commitment to God and the church right now? On a scale of one to ten (with ten being superterrific and one being very poor), how would you rate your commitment to the church? A ten? Really? Is your commitment superterrific? Or is it a seven or a six or a five? Or maybe a four? Let me ask it another way: If every member of our church had your level of commitment, what kind of church would we be? If every member of the church supported the church, served the church, loved the church, gave to the church just like you do, what kind of church would we be?

Are you giving your best? Could you do more? Could you help more? Could you contribute more? Could you be stronger in your commitment to the church? When the young Michelangelo announced that he wanted to become a sculptor, a master sculptor said to him, "My son, this will take your life," to which young Michelangelo answered, "What else is life for?"

Well, what else is life for but to be strong in our commitment to Christ, to be strong in our commitment to compassion, and to be strong in our commitment to the church?

12
The Attitude of Ownership

The Importance of Ownership

*S*O AGAIN *JESUS SAID TO THEM,* "VERY TRULY, *I TELL you, I am the gate for the sheep. All who came before me are thieves and bandits; but the sheep did not listen to them. I am the gate. Whoever enters by me will be saved, and will come in and go out and find pasture. The thief comes only to steal and kill and destroy. I came that they may have life, and have it abundantly.*

"I am the good shepherd. The good shepherd lays down his life for the sheep. The hired hand, who is not the shepherd and does not own the sheep, sees the wolf coming and leaves the sheep and runs away—and the wolf snatches them and scatters them. The hired hand runs away because a hired hand does not care for the sheep. I am the good shepherd. I know my own and my own know me, just as the Father knows me and I know the Father. And I lay down my life for the sheep. I have other sheep that do not belong to this fold. I must bring them also, and they will listen to my voice. So there will be one flock, one shepherd. For this reason the Father loves me, because I lay down my life in order to take it up again. No one takes it from me, but I lay it down of my own accord. I have power to lay it down, and I have power to take it up again. I have received this command from my Father."

—*John 10:7-18*

How long has it been since you had one of those terrific "light-bulb" moments, where suddenly, dramatically, without warning, the truth of God explodes into your life? It's one of these powerful moments of inspiration, when the curtains are pushed back, the fog clears, a new understanding dawns, a new perception leaps out at you, a new learning reverberates in your mind, a new insight captures your heart! The light bulb turns on!

I had a moment like that not long ago. I was in church on a Sunday morning, and as I read aloud that Scripture passage from John 10, it happened! I had read that Scripture a hundred times or more, but suddenly it came alive for me in a fresh, new way. That's what's so great about the Bible. It's so timeless, so relevant, so packed with meaning, so full of life. We think we know most everything there is to know about a certain passage, and we read along (reverently, but rather routinely), and then out of the blue it jumps up and surprises us so powerfully, when we least expect it.

It's like John Wesley, going to church that night at Aldersgate rather reluctantly, and then BANG! The truth of the Scriptures grabbed him, and his heart was strangely warmed.

It's like Moses, watching over his flock one day rather randomly, when suddenly the Word of God blared out of a burning bush, and Moses took off his shoes because he knew he stood on holy ground.

It's like Isaiah, who went into the Temple one morning rather casually, when surprise! He saw the Lord high and lifted up, and he heard God calling for a prophet and obediently responded: "Here am I; send me!" (Isaiah 6:8).

Well, that's the way it happens sometimes. God slips up on us. God's truth grabs us powerfully, and we wonder, "Why haven't I noticed this before?" That's the way I felt that Sunday morning as I read that passage from

John 10. Jesus is on his way to the cross and is speaking to his disciples, trying to prepare them for what is to come, trying to prepare them to take up the torch of his ministry after the Crucifixion and Resurrection. And he says: "I am the good shepherd. The good shepherd lays down his life for the sheep. The hired hand, who is not the shepherd and does not own the sheep, sees the wolf coming and leaves the sheep and runs away—and the wolf snatches them and scatters them. The hired hand runs away because a hired hand does not care for the sheep. I am the good shepherd . . . and I lay down my life for the sheep" (verses 11–15).

Not owning the sheep, the hired hand is indifferent; not owning the sheep, the hired hand couldn't care less; not owning the sheep, the hired hand thinks only of his self-interest; not owning the sheep, the hired hand runs away when the wolf comes to threaten the flock. But the good shepherd lays his life on the line for the flock. Why? Because he owns the sheep!

The point is clear. A sense of ownership is tremendously important! Don't misunderstand me; I'm talking about ownership, not in the sense of possessing something arrogantly or hoarding something selfishly or grabbing something greedily, but ownership in the sense of feeling responsibility for it, love for it, commitment to it! It's the kind of ownership a mother has for her child. I saw a young mother literally stop traffic last week.

She was only about twenty-seven years old and ninety-seven pounds, but she ran fearlessly into the middle of the street and commanded the traffic to stop—and it did! What gave her that power, that authority, that courage, that fearlessness? Simply this: Her child had broken away from her and had run out into the street. And she laid her life on the line to save her child. She ran out in front of cars and trucks on one of the busiest streets in America and made the traffic stop so she could save her child. That's the kind of ownership I'm talking about—the ownership of love and commitment, the ownership of caring and responsibility.

In recent years, the business world has discovered the importance of this sense of ownership. All good executives, motivators, and leaders know about this. It's hard to get people to do your job for you. They do best when they feel ownership in the project. You have to let them own the idea, own the dream.

Do you know the story about the reporter who saw some men working at a construction site? One man was working rather lazily. The reporter said, "What are you making?" He answered, "Four dollars an hour." A second man was working rather routinely. The reporter asked, "What are you making?" He answered, "Five dollars an hour." A third man was working enthusiastically, conscientiously, giving his heart and soul to it. The reporter asked him, "What are you making?" And he said, "A cathedral!"

The last man felt a sense of commitment, love, and responsibility. He had stock in what he was doing, pride in it—a sense of mission. He wasn't just going through the motions like those other workers. He wasn't just putting in his time like that hired man in John 10, who was ready to go over the hill at any moment if the wolf came or the going got rough. This man was committed to a dream. He was building a cathedral! He had ownership in it—a sense of mission and purpose.

This sense of ownership is important not only in the business world and in parenting. It is also extremely important in the spiritual world. Let me show you what I mean.

We Need a Sense of Ownership
with Regard to Our Own Personal Faith

We can ride on the coattails of others spiritually just so far and just so long, and then there comes a point where each of us has to take a stand—individually and personally. We have to have our own daily walk with God; our own personal relationship with Jesus Christ; our own sense of the Holy Spirit in our lives. No one else can do it for us.

We have to have our own personal prayer life, our own personal encounter with the Bible, our own theology, our own personal faith. Somewhere along the way, we have to figure out what we believe in, what we are committed to, what the real priorities are for us. We have to discover our own unique friendship with God. We can't just go through the motions or put in our time, or "play church." This is for keeps! Each of us has to make his or her own personal decision to give our life to God. Nobody else can do it for us. We have to have a sense of ownership in it.

Do you remember Florence Chadwick? She was a great distance swimmer, the first woman to swim the English Channel in both directions. On July 4, 1952, she entered the water off Catalina Island to swim the twenty-one miles to the California mainland. All went well at first, but the water was numbing cold, and then a thick fog rolled in—so thick as to obscure the support boats and the ever-present sharks, which were a constant threat. After sixteen hours of fighting the bone-chilling water and the dense fog, Florence Chadwick gave up and asked to be lifted from the water. Her support team urged her to keep trying because they were so close to the land (they could see it), and she was on a record pace; but disoriented by the fog and discouraged, she gave up and quit. When Chadwick got in the boat, she was disappointed with herself, because from that vantage point, she could see that her friends were right—the land was so close, just a few hundred yards away. She could have made it easily. Later she said to a reporter, "If I could have just seen the land for myself, I would have made it!" Later still, she made that swim in record time. The point is that her friends couldn't do it for her. They couldn't convince her. She needed to own it. She needed firsthand knowledge of it.

This brings to mind John Wesley at Aldersgate. He had been going through the motions, but there that night, it came to him, up close and personal. Here's how he described it: "I went very unwillingly to [Aldersgate, and there] I felt my heart strangely warmed. I felt I did trust in Christ, Christ alone for my salvation: And an assurance was given me, that he had taken away *my* sins, even *mine*, and saved *me* from . . . sin and death." Suddenly, Wesley felt a sense of ownership of his own personal faith. For years he had known that Christ had come for the world; now, suddenly, he realized that Christ had come for him, even him! He had known it all along intellectually in his head, but now he knew it personally, in his heart.

Some years ago, the noted concert violinist Itzhak Perlman was cornered in his dressing room by a stage mother. She insisted that he listen to a tape of her talented son, a violinist. Perlman was tired and didn't really want to listen to the tape, but the woman was so insistent, he relented. The woman switched on the portable tape player, and the music began. Immediately, Perlman was impressed. Such music! A difficult piece, but played with such insight and genius that it moved him to tears.

He listened, spellbound, to the entire recording and then composed himself before he spoke. "Madam, that was magnificent. How old is your son?"

"Eight years old," she said.

"Your son is eight years old and he made that tape?"

"Oh," said the mother, "that wasn't him. That was Jascha Heifitz, but all the neighbors think my son sounds just like him!"

We can't play somebody else's tape. We have to make our own tape. We need a sense of ownership of our own personal faith!

WE NEED A SENSE OF OWNERSHIP WITH REGARD TO THE CHURCH'S MINISTRY

What if every member felt a keen sense of commitment to and responsibility for the ministry of the church? What would that do to the church? to the world? That's what happened at Pentecost. The Holy Spirit came, and the disciples said, "Hey! We've got to do this!" They took up Christ's ministry and turned the world upside down.

When we join the church, we can't refer to it as "THEY" anymore. It's "WE"! Some people seem to think that clergypersons are supposed to be more committed to the church than are lay people. I don't buy that for a minute! We are all in this together. It's our church to share, both when things are rosy and when things are rough.

Do you remember the 1960s? There were tough times everywhere, and hard times in the church. I was serving a church in another state, and we were facing a very difficult problem. There was a lot of fear, panic, confusion— even hostility over this volatile problem. We put together a "blue-ribbon" committee. We studied the problem very carefully and then recommended to the board the correct Christian course of action. History has proved that the committee's decision was on target. But some that night in the board meeting didn't think so. The first four people to take the floor attacked harshly and bitterly, and all four ended their statement by saying, "If this board votes to do what this committee is recommending, I'm taking my family and my pledge and we are leaving!" It was an anxious moment, almost like a mob scene. Tension crackled in the air.

But then Walter Davis stood up. He was seventy-five years old at the time. He had thick, white hair, looking like a perfect blend of Mark Twain and Colonel Sanders. He spoke warmly but firmly: "I have two things to say. First, over the years, I've learned to trust our leaders. They're most always right. They have studied this with their bright minds and with their Christian spirits, and I'm going to vote with them. It's the right thing to do. Second, I want to say boldly that I'm not leaving our church, no matter how this turns out. I've been a member here for over sixty years. This church has done so much for me and my family. I've stayed with my church in the good times, and I'm not going to leave when the times are hard." When Walter Davis sat down, there was a moment of quiet reverence, and then the board did what it needed to do. It did the right thing, the Christian thing. We need a sense of ownership of the church's ministry like that, an ownership that stays solid through thick and thin, an ownership that doesn't run away when trouble comes.

WE NEED A SENSE OF GOD'S OWNERSHIP OF US

He owns it all and shares it with us. Remember how the psalmist put it:

> The earth is the LORD's and all that is in it,
>> the world, and those who live in it. (Psalm 24:1)
> For he is our God,
>> and we are the people of his pasture,
>> and the sheep of his hand. (Psalm 95:7)

This is really what the Christian faith is all about. It reminds us that we belong to God, that we need God, that we need a Savior and Redeemer. I looked up the word *redeem* in Webster's dictionary. Do you know what it says? "Redeem: to regain possession of." The hired hand loved only himself, and he deserted the flock, but the Good Shepherd so loved all the sheep that he put his life on the line for them. That's the good news of our faith. We belong to God, and God will never desert us, no matter what!

13
The Attitude of Hope
Rowing Against the Wind

*I*MMEDIATELY HE MADE THE DISCIPLES GET INTO THE *boat and go on ahead to the other side, while he dismissed the crowds. And after he had dismissed the crowds, he went up the mountain by himself to pray. When evening came, he was there alone, but by this time the boat, battered by the waves, was far from the land, for the wind was against them. And early in the morning he came walking toward them on the sea. But when the disciples saw him walking on the sea, they were terrified, saying, "It is a ghost!" And they cried out in fear. But immediately Jesus spoke to them and said, "Take heart, it is I; do not be afraid." Peter answered him, "Lord, if it is you, command me to come to you on the water." He said, "Come." So Peter got out of the boat, started walking on the water, and came toward Jesus. But when he noticed the strong wind, he became frightened, and beginning to sink, he cried out, "Lord, save me!" Jesus immediately reached out his hand and caught him, saying to him, "You of little faith, why did you doubt?" When they got into the boat, the wind ceased. And those in the boat worshiped him, saying, "Truly you are the Son of God."*

—Matthew 14:22-33

My brother, Bob, and I were just finishing up our long-distance telephone conversation. He is a minister in Memphis and has always been a great inspiration to me. As usual, I asked my traditional parting question: "Bob, what is the best sermon idea you have come up with lately?" (I need all the help I can get.) Quick as a flash, he responded, "Rowing Against the Wind." When I asked him to elaborate on the idea, he reminded me of that powerful story in the Gospels, when the disciples are caught in a storm out on the Sea of Galilee, being "battered by the waves, for the wind was against them."

As the disciples are rowing against the wind, scared, tired, frustrated, drained, depleted, Christ comes to them in an incredible way—"walking on the sea"! Isn't it fascinating that the presence of Christ is often most visible and most welcome when we are caught in a storm and rowing against the wind?

Remember this amazing story with me. It's a miracle story, but it is also a parable story. It's like a parable acted out. It deals with the frustration and helplessness we sometimes feel. It deals with the hard struggles of life. It deals with the overwhelming flood of problems that can rush in against us and pour down upon us. But it also reminds us that in the difficult moments—in the storms of life, those floodtide moments when we feel that we are about to be overcome and swept under—Christ comes to us in powerful and dramatic ways, bringing help and strength, peace and poise, confidence and victory.

Remember the context of the story. Jesus has just finished feeding the multitude with the five loaves and two fish. He has sent the crowd away, their bodies satisfied. Now he must feed himself, not with food for the body, but for his spirit. He sends the disciples ahead by boat to their next destination, while he goes up on a mountain to pray. In prayer and meditation, in thought and quiet time alone, he will again commune with his heavenly Father to recharge his spiritual life and renew the strength of his soul, in preparation for the new challenges he will soon face.

Now the disciples are out on the Sea of Galilee without him. The New Testament seems determined to call this famous body of water a "sea." Again and again, the writers call it the "Sea of Galilee." Actually, it's more like a lake. It's only about four and one-half miles wide and some seven miles long, but regardless of its small size, it could kick up a large-sized storm and could indeed be quite treacherous.

Winds could quickly come up, seemingly from nowhere, around those hills and stir the waves into a fury of rage and storm. In such a storm, the lake took on the threat of a big sea, and people on the water had to be very careful. Crossing the lake could be a simple venture if the wind were with you and your sails were turned to catch it. But if there were no wind, then you would have to row! You would have to put your muscle into it. Even then, the task (though not as pleasant as sailing) would have been manageable enough.

However, on this occasion in Matthew's Gospel, the disciples find themselves facing a number of difficult obstacles:

1. It is nighttime, and consequently, visibility is a real problem. They're out there in the dark.
2. It is cloudy because of the storm that is brewing. The disciples can't see the stars or follow them, so they are having trouble getting their sense of direction.
3. The wind of the storm is against them, so their sails are useless.
4. Not only do they have to row the boat, but they are rowing against the wind! They are rowing into the face

of the storm. They are not getting anywhere, not making much headway. The writer says that they are being "battered by the waves."

There they are, out there in the storm, being tossed to and fro, making no progress—tired, frustrated, drained, depleted, scared to death, confused, and probably a little miffed at Jesus for sending them out there. Where is the Master now? Where is he now, when we need him so desperately? We are tired, worn, defeated. We are in danger of being overwhelmed and drowned in the deep!

Can you identify with their plight? Can you relate? Don't we all have moments like that, when we feel stormed over and worn out? The storms and pressures of this world lash against us, and our Lord doesn't seem to be around. But look what happens—the Lord sees their dilemma. He is aware of their plight, and he goes straight toward them. He has been close by all along, closer even than they realized, and he comes to them. He comes to help them. He comes to save them. Through the wind, the storm, the danger, the chaos, the disorder, the disruption—he comes to them!

That's the way he comes to us, isn't it? He comes sometimes when we least expect him and most need him. He comes in the dead of night, in the thick of the storm, when it's darkest and most tumultuous—that's when he comes most vividly.

Look at the remarkable courage of Simon Peter here. "Lord, if it is you," he says, "command me to come to you on the water." Christ says, "Come," and Peter too walks on the water for a moment, but then his eyes go back to the winds and the waves, and fear takes over. He begins to sink. His Lord reaches over and pulls him out. And as they get into the boat, the storm subsides, the winds stop, and there is calm.

William Barclay has a fascinating comment on this story:

> See what happened. Immediately [when] Jesus saw His friends in trouble His own problems were set aside; the moment for prayer was past; the time for action had come; He forgot Himself and went to the help of His friends. That is the very essence of Jesus. The cry of human need to Him surpassed all other claims. His friends needed Him; He must go.
>
> What happened we do not know, and will never know. The story is cloaked in mystery which defies explanation. What we do know is that He came to them and their storm became a calm. With Him beside them nothing mattered anymore. . . . It is the simple fact of life, a fact which has been proved by countless thousands of men and women in every generation, that when Christ is there the storm becomes a calm, the tumult becomes a peace, the undoable becomes doable, the unbearable becomes bearable, and [people] pass the breaking point and do not break. To walk with Christ [will be] for us also the conquest of the storm. (*The Gospel of Mark;* page 163)

Now, with all this as a backdrop for our thinking, let's look at three important lessons that flow out of this dramatic story in Matthew 14.

WE ALL HAVE TO ROW AGAINST THE WIND SOMETIMES

It's a fact that life has its storms. Life is not an easy ride across a smooth, flat plateau. It gets bumpy sometimes. We all know that too well. There are mountaintops and valleys. Things don't always go just as we want them to go. Sometimes the winds blow against us. Sometimes we feel overwhelmed by the floodtides of life. Sometimes we feel burdened and crushed and weighted down. Sometimes we have to "row against the wind."

Recently, a man came into the office area of our church, looking for help. He was deeply troubled; you could tell it by looking at him. He looked worn and weary; his face was drawn; his eyes were tired, his expression was sad, and his shoulders were slumped over as if he were carrying a heavy load. Then, almost as if on cue, he said it: "I'm scared, worried, exhausted, depleted. I feel like I'm carrying hundred-pound weights on my back all the time. I am a burdened man." When he said that, he expressed what many people are feeling these days. Tremendously difficult problems "weigh down" upon us and threaten to crush the life out of us.

Think of it—inflation, depression, pollution, crime, fear, anxiety, grief, heartache, pressure, stress—we might just as well admit it. Life, for many people today, has become a strained and somber business. They feel heavy-laden, cast down, burdened. They feel as if they are caught in a storm and rowing against the wind.

Here is a place (the Scriptures tell us) where faith can help. We can cast our burdens on the Lord, and he will sustain us. If we will keep rowing, and look to him with the eyes of faith, he will come to our aid. He will come with strength and peace and confidence.

WHEN WE ARE IN THESE DIFFICULT "ROWING AGAINST THE WIND" SITUATIONS, CHRIST COMES TO US IN SPECIAL WAYS

If I were to ask you to recall those moments in your life when you felt God's presence most vividly, most dramatically, most powerfully, there might be a few who would recall a worship experience, or a few who would remember a joyous event or victorious moment. But most of us would remember how God came to us when we were "rowing against the wind," a time of sorrow or sadness, a time of tragedy or crisis, a time of sickness or injury, a time of misfortune or heartache.

Some years ago, some good friends of ours suddenly and tragically lost their youngest daughter. Her name was Ellen. She was sitting in the den at home one evening, laughing and talking with her mother. With no warning, her leg went numb, and then her arms. She fell back, paralyzed, and then, just as quickly, she was unconscious. She was rushed to the hospital, where all-night brain surgery was performed. She died the next day, sixteen years old. When I called to express my love and sympathy, Ellen's parents said, "God is giving us strength we didn't know we could have. He is holding us up and seeing us through this. We had Ellen for sixteen years, and she packed more life and love into sixteen years than most people do in a lifetime. We are all right. Don't worry about us, because God is with us. We can feel his presence nearer than breathing."

When we are "rowing against the wind," God comes in special ways to bring strength and help and hope.

In These Kinds of Situations, When Our Eyes Are Fixed on Christ, We Can Do Incredible Things, But When We Take Our Eyes Off Him, We Sink

Simon Peter looked at Christ, and he walked on water. When he took his eyes off Christ and looked at the waves, he became scared and began to sink.

Some years ago, John Redhead told about a little girl who was so excited because her father was going to take her to see the movie *Snow White.*

Someone said to the little girl, "But won't you be scared of the wicked witch?"

"No," she said. "When the witch comes on, I won't look at her. I'll just look at my father!" That's the way it works, isn't it? When we fix our eyes on God, we can do incredible things.

In Charlene Anderson's poem "Dialogue with God," God speaks first, insistent but with patient reassurance. And the poet answers, timid and afraid in the beginning, but with ultimate confidence and unconditional trust in the Lord:

Come out into the deep . . . But Lord, I'll sink to the bottom.

. . . .

I am with you . . . Okay, Lord, Here I come!

Epilogue
You Can Take Your Own Atmosphere with You

APPEAL TO YOU THEREFORE, BROTHERS AND SISTERS, by the mercies of God, to present your bodies as a living sacrifice, holy and acceptable to God, which is your spiritual worship. Do not be conformed to this world, but be transformed by the renewing of your minds, so that you may discern what is the will of God—what is good and acceptable and perfect.

—Romans 12:1-2

Not long ago, a television reporter was interviewing a group of astronauts about the opportunities and dangers of travel in space. He concluded the interview by asking this question: "What do you think is the single most important key to successful space travel?" One of the astronauts made an interesting response: "The secret of traveling in space is to take your own atmosphere with you!"

As I heard that, I realized this is also true in our travels through life on this earth. The key is to take your own atmosphere with you. We don't need to be changed or altered or influenced or destroyed by alien, or even hostile, environments in this life. We can take our own atmosphere with us. This is precisely what that magnificent passage in Paul's letter to the Romans is about, where Paul says

I appeal to you therefore, brothers and sisters, by the mercies of God, to present your bodies as a living sacrifice, holy and acceptable to God, which is your spiritual worship. Do not be conformed to this world, but be transformed by the renewing of your minds, so that you may discern what is the will of God—what is good and acceptable and perfect.

I like the way the J.B. Phillips Bible translates the last part: "Don't let the world around you squeeze you into its own mold." In other words, "Give your life totally to God and don't let anything change that or water that down or choke the life out of it!" Or, put yet another way, "You can take your own atmosphere with you." And what that really means is this: Attitude Is Your Paintbrush—It Colors Every Situation.

Study Guide
Attitude Is Your Paintbrush . . .
It Colors Every Situation

This study guide is designed for both individual and group use. When using the book individually, you may choose to read the entire book and then revisit each chapter as you make your way through the study guide. Or, if you prefer, you may take one chapter at a time, reading a chapter and then considering the questions provided for that chapter. In either case, you will find it helpful to record your responses and reflections in a notebook or journal.

When using the book in a group, you may choose one of the following study options, or create one of your own:

15-Week Study
One chapter per week, beginning with the introduction and ending with the epilogue.

13-Week Study
One chapter per week, including the introduction with chapter 1 and the epilogue with chapter 13.

12-Week Study
Week 1: Introduction and chapters 1–3. (Chapters 1–3 expound on the material included in the introduction.

Create your own study guide for this session by selecting from the questions provided.)

Weeks 2–11: Chapters 4–13

Week 12: Epilogue

9-Week Study
Week 1: Introduction

Week 2: Chapters 1–2

Week 3: Chapter 3

Weeks 4–8: Two chapters each week. (Condense the material by selecting from the study questions provided.)

Week 9: Epilogue

6-Week Study
Week 1: Chapters 1–3

Weeks 2–6: Two chapters per week. (Condense the material by selecting from the study questions provided.)

Optional: Incorporate material from the introduction and epilogue into weeks 1 and 6, respectively.

4-Week Study
Option 1 (A study of the entire book.)
Week 1: Introduction and chapters 1–3.

Weeks 2–3: Four chapters each week.

Week 4: Chapters 12–13 and the epilogue.

Option 2 (A study of selected chapters only.)
Week 1: Introduction and two chapters of your choice (other than chapters 1–3).

Weeks 2–4: Select any two additional chapters each week, including the epilogue with week 4.

Prior to your first session, determine who will serve as group leader. For this study, the leader's role is to facilitate discussion and encourage participation by all group members. To ensure fruitful discussion, *all participants* must commit to reading the designated chapter(s) before each group session. If open discussion is new or uncomfortable to your group, or if your time together is limited, it may be helpful for group members to reflect on the selected study questions prior to the session as well. Some may want to record their responses in a notebook or make brief notes in their books. (Note: Some questions may seem more appropriate for personal reflection than for group discussion. If members of your group are reluctant to discuss these questions, agree to reflect on them individually during the coming week.)

Introduction

1. How have you experienced the phrase spoken by Ann Turnage—"Attitude is your paintbrush; it colors every situation"—to be true in your own life? Think of a time recently when your attitude colored a particular situation. How did your attitude affect the situation? How might a different attitude have changed the situation?

2. Read Romans 12:2. How would you paraphrase this

passage for someone who is unfamiliar with the Christian faith? How would you explain what it means to "be transformed by the renewing of your mind"? Give an example from your own life, if possible.

3. Why do you think Paul urges us not to be conformed to this world? What does this advice have to do with one's attitude? What helps you to avoid the pitfall of conformity?

4. Read 1 Thessalonians 5:18. Do you know someone who gives thanks in all circumstances, even when his or her kindness is rejected? In what ways has this person been an inspiration to you or to others? What specific things can you do to follow this person's example and cultivate the attitude of gratitude in your own life?

5. Think of a time when you were experiencing a difficulty in a relationship—with a loved one, friend, coworker, or someone else. Did you try "the way of kindness"? If so, how did it help the situation? If not, how might a little kindness have changed the situation?

6. In what ways does your Christian faith give you confidence? How does confidence—or the lack of it—affect your attitude?

Chapter 1: The Attitude of Gratitude

1. What persons and experiences have helped you to learn the attitude of gratitude? How?

2. Read Luke 17:11-19. Why is it significant that the only leper who turned back and thanked Jesus was a Samaritan?

3. Who are the "outcasts" of our society? What relevance does this story from Luke have for us today?

4. Do you agree that the church is the best gift one can give to his or her children? Why or why not? Give examples from your own life or the lives of others, if possible.

5. Complete this sentence: If we didn't have the church, ...

6. What would life be like without *your* church—in your own life, in the life of your community, and in the life of the world? In other words, what "good" is your church doing in the lives of its members and of those in the community and world it serves? What else should your church be doing? What can you do to help make this happen?

7. Many people are "fair-weather Christians"; they never turn to faith until something "breaks" or goes wrong in their lives. What could you say to them about how to make the Christian faith a lifestyle—a part of their daily lives?

8. Have you ever been criticized or ridiculed for your Christian faith? What happened? How did you respond?

9. How would you define sacrificial love? Use one or more examples from your own life or the life of someone you know, if possible. What do Jesus Christ's life, death, and resurrection teach us about sacrificial love?

10. Complete this sentence: I am especially grateful for _____ because _____
_____. Now think of some way to express your gratitude to God today.

Chapter 2: The Attitude of Compassion

1. Many people think of compassion as having pity on someone, but compassion actually means "with heart"— reaching out to others with one's heart. With this definition in mind, describe at least one act of compassion you have witnessed or experienced this week.

2. This chapter suggests that compassion is self-giving, gracious, and active. What other characteristics would you use to describe compassion? What specific measures can we take to cultivate these characteristics in our lives?

3. Think about this statement for a moment: Any time we reach out to others in the gracious spirit of Christ, there is Holy Communion. What do you think this means? If possible, describe a time when you have had this kind of experience—whether you were giving or receiving.

4. Read Mark 5:24-34. How does Jesus demonstrate compassion in this story? What does this story teach us about how we are to show compassion in our world today?

5. This story in Mark is only one example of Jesus' compassionate spirit. Scan the Gospels (Matthew, Mark, Luke, John) to find other stories in which Jesus shows compassion by reaching out in love to others. What do these stories have in common? What recurring message or lesson do we find in them?

6. Using the definition that compassion is "active love," how compassionate are you? How compassionate is your church/group? Acts of compassion can be both spontaneous and planned. Challenge yourself to look for one opportunity each day this week to reach out *sponta-*

neously in active love. Now think of at least one new way that you—and/or your church/group—can *plan* to reach out in active love, and take steps to make it happen!

Chapter 3: The Attitude of Confidence

1. Read Matthew 8:5-10. Why was Jesus so impressed by the centurion's faith? Like the centurion, we too live in a "seeing is believing" world. In what ways do we demonstrate our faith to others? What can we do to increase our faith and drive out doubt and fear? Give examples from your own life, if possible.

2. This chapter suggests that the Bible is an "instruction manual" for living a meaningful life. How would you describe the Bible and its purpose to someone who has never read or heard any part of it? What would you say about its importance in your own life? How has it been a source of direction, comfort, inspiration, and strength?

3. Why is Bible study important to Christian discipleship? What methods of Bible study have you found to be effective in your own Christian walk? What benefits have you experienced in individual or private Bible study? in group study?

4. How can we make a credible case that Christianity can fill the spiritual hunger of our day? What specific things can we do as the church and as individual Christians to meet that spiritual hunger?

5. Respond to this statement: Christianity is not just good for society; it is the truth. How can we demonstrate the truth of the Christian faith?

6. In what ways are we as Christians to love the church with Christ as its head? How will others know that we truly love the church? What signs of our love should be evident?

7. Think of a time when you were reluctant to turn to God and trust in God. What happened? Read Proverbs 3:5-6. When have you experienced the truth of these verses?

Chapter 4: The Attitude of Determination

1. In your own words, explain what it means to strive first for the kingdom of God. What happens when you put God first in your life?

2. Is it always possible to tell if someone has a strong relationship with God? Why or why not? What are some of the signs or evidences of such a relationship?

3. When are the times you feel closest to God? What strengthens your relationship with God?

4. Read Exodus 20:12. What does this commandment mean? What outcome is promised for those who abide by this commandment? What message does this commandment have for us today?

5. Read Ephesians 6:1-4. What help can we find in these verses for building strong Christian families? What does it mean to bring up our children "in the discipline and instruction of the Lord" (verse 4)? What else do you believe helps to build a strong family?

6. What can we do as individuals, as families, and as the

body of Christ to help strengthen the families of our nation?

7. Why is it important for Christians to be involved in the church? What things does the church do for us? What things are we to do for the church? Why do *you* need the church?

Chapter 5: The Attitude of Humility

1. Whose "shoulders" have helped to carry you through life? In other words, what persons have supported and strengthened you the most—in the past as well as the present? How? What have you done—or could you do—to show them how much their support means to you?

2. Read Matthew 6:14-15; Matthew 18:21-35; and Ephesians 4:31-32. What do these verses tell us about forgiveness? What do God's grace and the power of the Holy Spirit have to do with our ability to forgive others?

3. How would you define or explain unconditional love? John 3:16 tells us of the ultimate example of unconditional love. What other examples of unconditional love are there in the Bible?

4. When has the Holy Spirit enabled you to love someone you found difficult to love? Tell about that experience.

5. What is the purpose or calling of the church? What role does the Holy Spirit play in building or strengthening the church to fulfill this calling?

6. What specific things can we do as individual church members and as the collective church body to ensure that

the Holy Spirit is leading and empowering us? What are the signs of a Spirit-led church?

Chapter 6: The Attitude of Perseverance

1. Read 2 Timothy 4:6-8. "Keep the faith" has become a popular saying of our time, meaning to be faithful to a cause or individual or group. What did Paul mean when he said he had "kept the faith"?

2. Read Matthew 16:24-25; Luke 9:62; 14:33; and John 12:25-26. What do these verses tell us about what it means to be truly committed to Jesus Christ? What things threaten to weaken or break our commitment? What can we do to overcome these temptations and distractions?

3. What is your definition of Christian love? In what ways can we share the sacrificial love of Jesus Christ with the world? What are some specific ways *you* have found to do this?

4. What does it mean to put love first in your life? What does this require?

5. Christians through the ages have had to deal with competing ideas, causes, and philosophies, all vying for their attention, energy, and resources. What are some of the competing beliefs and practices that we Christians are confronted with today? How should we respond? Give an example from your own life or the life of someone you know, if possible.

6. What helps you to be true to the Christian faith, to persevere in your daily faith walk?

Chapter 7: The Attitude of Open-mindedness

1. What does it mean to be open-minded? Why do you think some Christians believe that open-mindedness is a threat to Christianity? Do you agree or disagree? Why?

2. What is the difference between open-mindedness and tolerance? In what way are we called to be tolerant as Christians? Is it ever appropriate for us to be intolerant? When?

3. Think of a time when you were threatened by a new idea, person, or way of doing something. What did you do? Were you able to overcome your closed-mindedness? If so, how?

4. Do you agree that having a closed mind is sinful? Why or why not?

5. How does the fear of change contribute to closed-mindedness? Read Isaiah 40:31; Matthew 28:20; and Romans 8:31-39. How can these verses help us when we are confronted with change? What other promises can we find in the Bible to help us overcome our fears?

6. How were the teachings of Christ a "new approach" to the people of his day? In what way is the law of love a new approach in our own day?

7. Read 2 Corinthians 5:17. What does it mean to be a new creation? How does the new life that Christ gives enable us to be open-minded?

Chapter 8: The Attitude of Joy

1. Read Philippians 4:4-5. What does it mean to "rejoice in the Lord"? Is it possible to do this *always*, as Paul instructs? Why or why not?

2. Now read Philippians 4:6-7. How is prayer related to our ability to be joyful? Do you believe it is possible for someone to have the peace of God and not be joyful? Why or why not?

3. Read John 15:11. What is the difference between happiness and the joy that comes from Christ?

4. Read Nehemiah 8:10. When have you experienced joy despite suffering or sadness? What enabled you to be joyful? What gave you strength?

5. Find the words *rejoice, joy,* and *joyful* in a Bible concordance and look up several passages containing each word. (Include verses from both the Old and New Testaments.) What do these passages tell us about joy? about the nature of God? about our relationship with Jesus Christ? Choose two or three of your favorite verses and write each on an index card, or commit them to memory. Read or recite them regularly to increase your joy.

6. Read Luke 5:27-32. Why do you think the Pharisees and scribes were disturbed that Jesus was "having a good time"? Why was Jesus socializing with such a disreputable crowd? What message might this story have for us today?

7. This chapter gives several examples of persons who have possessed the joy that is our Christian heritage. What

----

examples can you think of—from the Bible, from the pages of history, or from your own life? How have these persons demonstrated that Christianity is a radiantly joyful faith?

Chapter 9: The Attitude of Faith

1. Read Mark 1:14-20. Why do you think Simon, Andrew, James, and John stopped what they were doing, left everything behind, and immediately followed Jesus? How do you think they were able to do that?

2. What does it mean to be a fisher of people for Jesus Christ?

3. How would you respond to someone who says that the only things worthy of our trust are those things that can be proven scientifically? How would you explain your faith, your ability to trust in God?

4. When was the most recent time you have taken a risk—a leap of faith—in order to follow Christ? What did it require of you? What was at stake? What happened? How were you aware of God's faithfulness to you?

5. Read Luke 17:33 (see also Matthew 10:39; 16:25; Mark 8:35; Luke 9:24; and John 12:25-26). The second part of this verse is a paradox. What does it mean? In what way must you "lose your life" in order to save it? What sacrifices or risks is Christ asking *you* to make for his sake and the sake of the gospel?

6. Read James 2:26. What does this verse mean? What kind of works are we called to do as followers of Christ?

----

7. Think about these questions during the coming week: How can others see that I am a Christian? What are the evidences of my faith in my daily life? Determine what changes you need to make in order to become a better disciple of Jesus Christ.

Chapter 10: The Attitude of Trust

1. Read Acts 19:1-7. In what ways were the disciples in Ephesus changed by the Holy Spirit? How has the power of the Holy Spirit changed your life? In what ways have these changes required you to trust in God?

2. In what way does our ability to forgive others require trust? How does God's Holy Spirit work through us when we forgive others? Give an example from your own life, if possible.

3. Read Ephesians 6:10; 2 Timothy 2:1; 1 Peter 4:11; and Colossians 1:11. What do these verses promise us? Why, then, can we be confident as Christians? To what degree do you think a person's confidence is determined by his or her ability to trust God?

4. Think of a time when you trusted God to give you confidence. What happened?

5. Read 1 Corinthians 15:54-57. What is our victory as Christians? In what way is trust a prerequisite of this victory?

6. Read 1 John 5:4. How does our Christian faith enable us to "conquer the world"?

Chapter 11: The Attitude of Commitment

1. Read 2 Timothy 2:1-11. How does the grace of God that is ours in Christ Jesus give us strength? Give an example from your own life, if possible.

2. What meaning does verse three have for your life? How have you shared in suffering, and how has the strength of Christ seen you through these times of trial?

3. Read 1 Corinthians 13. What, in your opinion, is the most important message of this familiar chapter? How would you summarize this message in one sentence?

4. What does it mean for us as Christians to be committed to love and compassion? Give several examples of persons you know whose lives demonstrate this commitment.

5. Reread 2 Timothy 2:8-11. What underlying message does Paul have for Timothy in these verses? Why was it important for Timothy to remain strong in his commitment to the church? Why is it important for *us* to do the same?

6. Reread the last section of this chapter. Then think carefully about this question: On a scale of one to ten (with ten being strong and one being weak), how would you rate your commitment to the church right now? Answer as honestly as you can. What specific things can you do to strengthen your commitment to the church? Pray about this during the coming week.

Chapter 12: The Attitude of Ownership

1. Read John 10:7-18. What does this image of the good

149

shepherd tell us about Jesus' love for us and commitment to us? In what ways are we also called to be good shepherds—dedicated shepherds—rather than hired hands?

2. How is a sense of ownership important to our growth as Christians? What gives you a sense of ownership in the Christian faith?

3. Read Ephesians 4:11-13. What is "the work of ministry" to which Paul refers in verse twelve? What does it mean to have a sense of ownership in this ministry? Why is this important to the church's ability to fulfill its mission?

4. Do you have a sense of ownership in the ministry of *your* church? Why or why not? What would increase your ownership in the church and its ministry? What can you do to help make this happen? Pray about this during the coming week.

5. Read Psalm 24:1-2 and Psalm 95:1-7. What do these verses tell us about God and God's relationship with us? How are we to respond?

6. How does belonging to God give us a sense of protection? In what way does it also give us a sense of freedom?

Chapter 13: The Attitude of Hope

1. Read Matthew 14:22-33. How is this story a parable for our own lives?

2. Think of a time when you felt as if you were "rowing against the wind." What were your fears during that time?

What gave you hope? How did you make it through the storm?

3. Peter's faith wavered when he took his eyes off Jesus and focused on the waves around him. What causes your faith to waver? What helps you to keep your eyes "fixed on Jesus"?

4. Read Matthew 17:18-20; Mark 11:23-24; and Luke 12:28. What do these verses tell us about doubt? about the power of faith?

5. Read Romans 5:1-5. According to these verses, what gives us hope? How does suffering increase our hope and, therefore, our faith?

6. When have you felt God's presence most powerfully in your life? What do those experiences have in common? How did you experience God in a special way during those times? How did those experiences increase your hope and your faith?

Epilogue

1. Read Romans 12:1-2; recall that this passage was also used in the introduction. Have your thoughts about these verses changed in any way during the course of this study? If so, how?

2. Describe the kind of atmosphere in which you would like to spend the rest of your life. What can *you* do to create this atmosphere and take it with you wherever you go?

3. Of the thirteen attitudes highlighted in this book, which

seem to come more easily for you? Which attitudes are more difficult for you? Why do you think this is so? What can you do to cultivate these attitudes in your daily life?

Study guide written by Sally D. Sharpe.